POLITICAL TRADITIONS IN FOREIGN POLICY SERIES
Kenneth W. Thompson, Editor

The values, traditions, and assumptions undergirding approaches to foreign policy are often crucial in determining the course of a nation's history. Yet, the interconnections between ideas and policy for landmark periods in our foreign relations remain largely unexamined. The intent of this series is to encourage a marriage between political theory and foreign policy. A secondary objective is to identify theorists with a continuing interest in political thought and international relations, both younger scholars and the small group of established thinkers. Only occasionally have scholarly centers and university presses sought to nurture studies in this area. In the 1950s and 1960s the University of Chicago Center for the Study of American Foreign Policy gave emphasis to such inquiries. Since then the subject has not been the focus of any major intellectual center. The Louisiana State University Press and the series editor, from a base at the Miller Center of Public Affairs at the University of Virginia, have organized this series to meet a need that has remained largely unfulfilled since the mid-1960s.

SCHOOLS OF THOUGHT
IN INTERNATIONAL RELATIONS

SCHOOLS OF THOUGHT IN INTERNATIONAL RELATIONS

INTERPRETERS, ISSUES, AND MORALITY

KENNETH W. THOMPSON

LOUISIANA STATE UNIVERSITY PRESS

BATON ROUGE AND LONDON

05 04 03 02 01 00 99 98 97 96   5 4 3 2 1

Designer: Rebecca Lloyd Lemna
Typeface: Galliard
Typesetter: Impressions Book and Journal Services, Inc.
Printer and binder: Thomson-Shore, Inc.

Library of Congress Cataloging-in-Publication Data

Thompson, Kenneth W., 1921–
    Schools of thought in international relations : interpreters,
issues, and morality / Kenneth W. Thompson.
        p.   cm. — (Political traditions in foreign policy series)
    Includes index.
    ISBN 0-8071-2097-9 (cloth : alk. paper). — ISBN 0-8071-2131-2
(pbk. : alk. paper)
    1. International relations—Philosophy.   2. International
relations—Moral and ethical aspects.   I. Title.   II. Series.
JX1395.T529   1996
327—dc20   96-26852
                                                            CIP

To my children

Kenneth C.
Paul A.
James D.
Carolyn A.

CONTENTS

PREFACE

At first glance, the publication of another book on political theory and international-relations thinking may appear redundant—and ill-timed. New approaches and schools of thought are mushrooming as I draft this preface. I know of a department in which a group of young scholars recently prepared a syllabus and worked up an outline for a scope and methods course. As they completed the task, they found they had identified no fewer than nineteen separate theories and approaches. Evidently, announcing in an article or a lecture that one is providing the world of scholarship with a new theoretical perspective is sufficient to bring legitimacy to a theory. In this sense, a contribution by a recent Ph.D. is no different from works that survive after two thousand years of discussion and debate.

The trend to which I point is new. As a student, administrator, and professor for half a century, I have witnessed recurring debates over theories and approaches. If memory serves, the process in every instance was remarkably similar. For example, the appearance of the approach that seeks to promote international organization goes back to an intense debate in the Congress over the League of Nations and the growth of international institutions. Scholars trace its origins not only to the American architect of a league to enforce the peace, Woodrow Wilson, but to a host of his predecessors, authors of peace plans, such as Erasmus, Eméric Cruce, the Duc de Sully, the Abbé de Saint-Pierre, William Penn, and Jeremy Bentham. Theories of international law began with Hugo Grotius and continued through Francisco de Vitoria, Eméric Vattel, Lassa Oppenheim, J. L. Brierly,

Charles de Visscher, and Quincy Wright. Much the same can be said about economic theories and ideas of interdependence going back to Adam Smith, Richard Cobden, Karl Marx, Joseph Schumpter, and most recently, contemporary interdependence theorists. As for international politics, the growth and development of political realism is traceable to Augustine, Machiavelli, Bismarck, Max Weber, Friedrich Nietszche, Nicholas Spykman, George Kennan, Louis Halle, Reinhold Niebuhr, and Hans J. Morgenthau.

To equate the most recent propositions by relative newcomers to the study of international relations with the ideas of major thinkers whose writings have survived the test of time seems questionable on its face. It demonstrates a certain naïveté and lack of seriousness by those who make the claim, as well as an ignorance of intellectual history. It can lead to a discrediting of theory as a disciplined activity proceeding through discrete stages of development and involving an intensive process of review and criticism. If I assert tomorrow that nations in the post–Cold War era need pay no heed to the imperatives of national security, I hardly deserve the same attention reserved for Hans Morgenthau, Reinhold Niebuhr, and Nicholas Spykman.

Because of the lack of intellectual discrimination in the recognition of international-relations theories, the discipline runs the risk of losing its way. It suffers from aimless and random experimentation and fascination with anything that is novel. The latest fad or fashion takes over, and historic and traditional approaches are pushed into the background. Ironically, efforts that are intended to advance the prestige of the field have the opposite effect. Dialogue takes on the character of the Tower of Babel. Specialists can no longer talk with one another or read one another's journals. At one moment, a group may take control of a professional society and oftentimes the editorial preferences and policy of its journal. With the coming of an inevitable backlash, another group takes over. Scholarly discourse yields to majority votes, but any triumph is transient because it is built on sand. There is a short-term, shot-in-the-dark character to theories that are the product of hurried formulation. They come and go and do little to advance knowledge.

In the present volume, I discuss schools of thought and approaches that have had a longer life than the nineteen separate theories earlier mentioned. These traditional approaches constitute a coherent body of thought that has both empirical and logical validity. Theorists and practitioners have joined in the development of the theory behind them. For over a half century in the contemporary world, critical thinkers have raised issues that require clarification and explanation. Arguments have been joined about the philosophy and the assumptions underlying certain theories. In this book, I review the origins of the more traditional approaches to politics and diplomacy and concentrate attention on some of the ethical issues posed by the approaches. The contributions of the foremost representatives of the major schools of thought are studied. The leading figures are both philosophers and pundits. I suggest that consensus has been reached on some of the questions and issues with which each school is concerned, while others remain unresolved. Finally, I undertake to evaluate questions that involve realism, idealism, and cynicism as they affect presidents, television, the public, and the United Nations.

ACKNOWLEDGMENTS

No one can properly thank all those who have contributed to his thinking and development. For me, an unnumbered host of close friends and chance associates have helped shape my view of politics, ethics, and diplomacy. I have often been the beneficiary of a brilliant lecture, a casual observation in a forgotten conversation, or a powerful intervention in a Ph.D. examination. I know no way of thanking all those who threw new light on my struggle to gain understanding.

A long procession of tutors and professors have left the imprint of their thinking and philosophy on my mind, and I dedicated *Masters of International Thought* to five of them. They were my college teachers, and it was in college that I discovered what it meant to be a master teacher. I still renew my intellectual kinship with them whenever I face an especially difficult problem.

Graduate school was a tale of two giant figures in international relations at the University of Chicago. Not so much to memorialize as to help others understand what each brought to the field, I discuss them in the first half of Chapter I. None of us who were students after World War II could have found our way without Hans J. Morgenthau and Quincy Wright. They shaped the field of international relations for generations to come.

When I left academia for a time to enter the foundation world, I had my baptism of fire in the theory and practice of politics and foreign policy. I had the good fortune to work for a former Rhodes Scholar and college dean who was to become secretary of state. He taught me to strive for perspective and patience and how to manage affairs with difficult associates and importuners. For me, he retains an image that bears little relationship to his public image. Another friend was America's foremost practical theologian, whose understanding of man and politics has to this day not been matched. I write about him in Chapter II and elsewhere throughout this book.

Last but not least, my students at the University of Virginia and coworkers at the Miller Center brought me a special opportunity that exceeded all previous experience. Few who have never taught—and there are many in the halls of our legislatures—can comprehend the bonds that develop between students and their teachers over a semester, a year, or an entire career. To observe students' unfolding interest, to sense their intellectual and moral growth, to make an all-too-modest contribution to their understanding—these things bind faculty and students together as perhaps no other relationship can do. Nor can any profession give one quite the rewards of working on substantive programs with colleagues and devoted secretaries and administrators.

Having said all this, I must refer my readers to the dedication page. Life is a struggle for young and old, and it must always be so. To draw ever closer in later years to a family however distant is a kind of Protestant nirvana, not because it brings peace and tranquility but because in those years the essential has a way of taking over from the trivial.

I have not given names in my acknowledgments—or only a few—in part because one's deepest joys and friendships are a private matter, a unique personal experience and a memory forever. For those who would know some of those whom I have acknowledged, I invite you to read the pages that follow. If I fail to mention my parents, it is because I know that I owe everything in life to them and to their memory—Agnes and Thor C. Thompson.

A thousand words cannot describe the countless ways my executive secretary makes possible the completion of each day's work at the Miller Center. Moreover, my profound appreciation goes to those colleagues who have gone out of their way to serve the Center and me beyond the call of duty—who will know the gratitude I feel without my ever mentioning their names, as will my friends and contributors to what we have tried to do together to move the Center toward the goals of the donor. I owe a great deal to a brilliant young graduate student/editor who brought remarkable skills to her task. Last, I thank my wife, who sacrificed time we might have spent together to make possible what would otherwise have been impossible. Only someone who is herself a teacher-scholar would have tolerated such long hours of isolation.

SCHOOLS OF THOUGHT
IN INTERNATIONAL RELATIONS

INTRODUCTION

In one respect, this book is an inquiry into intellectual history. Its goal is to offer a perspective on international studies: its origins, changes, developments, and present status. Looking back, what were its beginnings and who were the founders? What are some of the factors responsible for continuity and change? Are there any enduring and unifying ideas that have been sustained over time? Who are the interpreters whose writings have endured?

In any field or discipline, the questions that are asked at each stage along the way are indicators of fundamental concerns. They help us plot the history of the discipline and explain how it arrived at its present state. The "great debates" that occur periodically between the spokesmen of contending viewpoints also perform an important role in elucidating approaches. In the pages that follow, we set about gathering empirical and logical evidence to describe and evaluate important schools of thought.

In the late 1940s and 1950s, observers and scholars asked if the study of international relations was a recognized discipline. Did it have a unifying focus? Was it based on some informing principle? Did it address certain basic, recurrent, and defining questions? Economics as a field of study has such a focus, and so does political science. Frederick Dunn, the leader of the renegade group that moved from Yale to Princeton, argued that international relations required the study of twenty separate disciplines. In his monumental work *The Study of War*, Quincy Wright sought to collaborate with specialists whose fields ranged from agriculture to zoology. In his graduate lectures he dealt with social trends from anomie to xenophobia. International relations was interdisciplinary in character because of its wide-ranging subject matter, but few were prepared to call it a discipline.

Later, Wright and others went on to explore competing definitions and unifying themes. They examined community and society as possible unifying concepts and technology and industry as determinants of the field. What was the impact of technological change on the scope and content of the field? Subsequently, the process of modernization was considered. What were its transforming effects on the study of international relations? In time, nationalism, ethnicity, and social movements became objects of study. In what ways did their study require a reformulation of the subject? Only in the late 1940s did a unifying theme emerge as students turned to international politics as a central focus.

In every discipline, there is a tendency to imagine the latest development is the best. For basic science and technology, the weight of evidence largely confirms and supports this viewpoint. In the humanities and social sciences, the evidence is far less compelling. Changes that apparently require new methodologies and paradigms, which resourceful entrepreneurs produce on demand, have had mixed success. Striking new concepts and approaches all have their day. History moves on, and others take their place. The evaluation of new knowledge is an ongoing process of sifting out false starts and clever designs from enduring legacies that will stand the test of time.

The starting point for the present study is a survey of three of the earliest schools of thought, located at Chicago, Harvard, and Yale. Although some may quarrel with this selection, they may at the same time agree that choosing the leading institutions of the 1940s was a far simpler task than attempting to do the same for the 1990s. Chicago, Harvard, and Yale prevailed in part because of early institutional commitments and pioneering thinkers, as well as the overall quality of the universities. Their strengths reflected more than the achievements and prestige of their institutions. Leadership in international studies at each university was an important factor. The University of Chicago in particular flourished because of two intellectual giants—Hans J. Morgenthau and Quincy Wright. The influence of the three schools increased after World War II and continued even after their leadership came into question. (The leaders at Chicago moved to other institutions, Morgenthau to the City University of New York and Wright to the University of Virginia, where they continued to teach.) Harvard had an array of talented professors, but no one equaled Morgenthau's and Wright's authority in the field. Harvard's strengths were its name, an impressive general faculty, and its first-rate students. Yale recruited a cadre of scholars more numerous than Chicago's but at the time of lesser standing. Then the entire Yale group, with the exception of Arnold Wolfers, migrated en masse to Princeton.

To characterize these three programs as "schools of thought" may appear more European than American. In Europe over the years, one has heard repeated references to the Heidelberg School, the Frankfurt School, the Austrian School, and so on. Individuals were identified with institutional centers and schools of thought. Some were founders of a particular approach. American parallels existed, however; institutions became identified with leaders and approaches. It is fitting, therefore, in a discussion of the origins of international-relations scholarship and teaching, to identify Morgenthau and Wright with the Chicago School and to associate a political-theory emphasis with the Harvard School. One can do this without confusing the structure of the American university system with that of Europe. Each of the three American institutions bequeathed a distinct approach and informing theory to the field. Acceptance of their work gained strength from the intellectual atmosphere of the university at which they taught. For the University of Chicago, the Morgenthau/ Wright era was a golden age in international studies. With GI's returning from military service around the world, the time was ripe. It was a time of intellectual ferment that was not to be seen again for generations. The intensity of the dialogue between mature students and outstanding professors was unique and memorable.

Beginning in the late 1970s, the focus began to shift to normative questions in international relations. Students turned their attention from themes of national interest and national power to issues of international morality or ethics. To the extent scholars had previously discussed international morality, it was with reference to international law and institutions. There were exceptions, such as Morgenthau, who throughout his career was concerned with international morality as related to national interest. Most of the writings from the 1930s

3

to the 1950s had equated morality with the growth of international law and institutions. Publicists and scholars tended to write of *good internationalism* and *bad nationalism*. Convictions and a guilty conscience combined to drive such thinking. Americans who had turned their backs on the League of Nations now embarked on an internationalist crusade to guarantee that history would not repeat itself. Few bothered to consider examples of *bad internationalism,* such as the Communist International, and *good nationalism,* which took the form of representative government.

The major impetus toward reconsidering normative questions came from a few towering figures who understood both the harsh nature of world politics and the possibilities and limits of international morality. Foremost among the group was a Protestant theologian, Reinhold Niebuhr, who is discussed in Chapter II. He dominated the discussion of political ethics from the late 1940s until the time of his death. He commanded the respect of both religious and secular thinkers. After one conference in which both participated, Walter Lippmann was overheard asking, "How many generations will it be before we see his equal?" From conservatives to liberals, from intellectuals to political and business leaders, no one could ignore Niebuhr. He opened up a dialogue between idealists and realists that had languished since the 1930s. He attended the conferences of political scientists and internationalists; the sheer weight of his intellectual and personal power commanded respect. He was not the only thinker to come before such groups, but Niebuhr was by far the most imposing figure, and no one could forget the impression he made.

It would be wrong to overlook the pundits and the diplomatists who contributed to this book by bringing theory and practice together. Indeed, it may be a sign that America is coming of age when intellectuals and students are reaching beyond the boundaries of academia to gain new insights on ethics and foreign policy. Two of those who have contributed—George F. Kennan and Paul H. Nitze—have recently written their memoirs. Kennan has added to his earlier and more extensive *Memoirs* with two volumes, one a collection of his earlier writings entitled *At a Century's Ending: Reflections, 1982–1995* and the other, *Around the Cragged Hill: A Personal and Political Philosophy.* The distinguishing characteristic of the latter volume is its emphasis on political philosophy and ethics, and foreign policy in particular. It also includes Kennan's reflections on human nature. Kennan's successor as director of the U.S. State Department's Policy Planning Staff, Paul Nitze, has written an intellectual autobiography of his own. *Tension Between Opposites* is based partly on his experience in organizing a political-theory course at the School for Advanced International Studies. I have attempted to appraise the contributions that the two diplomatists have made in normative thinking by analyzing their writings under the headings of science and politics, man and human nature, and ethics and foreign policy. In some areas they agree; in others, for example, science and politics and their views of human nature, they differ. Where ethics are concerned, however, the most revealing difference is clearly between Niebuhr and the two diplomatists, illustrating both the possibilities and the limits of the practitioner's approach to philosophical issues.

Chapter III is devoted to outstanding issues representing points of difference affecting attitudes, orientations, and philosophies. What are the prevailing attitudes toward peace and war, and are they compatible or always in conflict? For example, optimism is vital in American politics. Often it spells the difference between victory and defeat for a candidate. Yet realism is also a decisive factor in domestic and international politics. How do the two attitudes relate? Must they forever be viewed as opposite? When do they come together, and what are the points of convergence? Is anyone consistently optimistic or realistic? What are the strengths and weaknesses of these two stances? In what ways can one of the two balance the insufficiencies of the other? If they are, in effect, paired opposites, can they sometimes serve to reinforce each other? Although commentators and lecturers often use words such as *optimism,* the purpose of our discussion is to accord it and other attitudes the serious analysis they deserve.

The relation between theory and practice poses another question. If we assume each represents a particular professional attitude or posture, what are the prospects for reducing, if not eliminating, the gulf that has grown up between them? Are theorists and practitioners destined to remain in two separate worlds, or can they be united? I have experienced life in both—for a decade in the academy as graduate student and faculty member, for nearly twenty years as an officer in a large foundation directing wide-ranging international programs, and, finally, for twenty years as a professor and director of a public-affairs institute in a highly regarded university. In each position, I have felt the tension between the two professional stances. Because of my allegiance to *both* theory and practice, I have never been entirely at home in either world. I have grown familiar with the practitioners' charge that theoretical work is irrelevant and "merely talk." In a university setting, I have sometimes felt the scorn that scholars can heap on administrators and policymakers. Because of my concern that both theory and practice run the risk of professional deformation, I continue to believe in the inescapable interdependency of the two as a means of closing the gap. Theorists—acknowledged or not—who divorce themselves totally from practice become the victims of self-indulgent abstractionism. Practitioners and policymakers who have only contempt for theorists forget the words of John Maynard Keynes: that behind every policy initiative is the work of some "academic scribbler."

Finally, force and peace are often seen as paired opposites; proponents rarely recognize their necessary connection in realism. Once again, the issue is whether we concede that the two opposites must meet and coexist in the end. Deterrence of potential force kept the peace for a half century during the Cold War. "Peace through strength" became the watchword for American and Soviet policy. The old military adage that warriors cannot sit on their bayonets suggests that the means of force can sometimes bring conflict. Unsheathed weapons are there to be used. In this instance, however, as in others, paired opposites can merge. Force and peace are parts of a strategic whole. Political realism creates the connective tissue: "We must negotiate from strength."

Following a discussion of optimism, practice, and peace, the book's attention shifts to an examination of the quest for a new world order. During the Gulf War, President George Bush revived the American vision of a new international order, a concept with a long history. Since his declaration, the signs of progress have been few. Yet the need for a more effective international order is only too evident in crisis points around the globe: Bosnia, Cuba, Haiti, Israel and Palestine, North Korea, China, Taiwan. But genuine progress remains halting at best. For a brief moment in 1992, the image of nations joining together in war in defense of a common purpose seemed to point the way toward change. The euphoria surrounding a new world order, however, could have been held within bounds if observers had remembered the state-centered orientation of nations. First, the United Nations, heralded as an advance toward a new world order, remains subject to the will of its member nations. Second, the philosophical and political orientation of leaders has driven what progress has been made toward a new world order. Then-president Bush, formerly U.S. ambassador to the United Nations, proclaimed world order as a relevant goal. Woodrow Wilson was the world's prophet for a league to enforce the peace. Jimmy Carter defended a new world order for human rights. In their zeal these men strayed from reality, but their orientations obviously influenced public opinion for the long run, if not national policy in the short run. The journey remains long and difficult. The gap between policy proclamations and the actual foreign policies of nations has not been closed. Moreover, scholarly analysis and policymaking respond to widely different assumptions and conclusions.

Finally, we address political philosophy and the interrelationships of realism, liberalism, and socialism. Early in the Cold War, John H. Herz wrote a pioneering study of liberalism and realism in which he explored the interdependence of the two. Herz asked how the harsher aspects of realism could be justified in the light of the liberal creed. In the 1930s, the British historian E. H. Carr challenged conventional thinking in his work *The Twenty Years' Crisis* and followed it with an analysis of socialism and realism and "the conditions of peace." The importance of these studies stems from the authors' determination to explore the interconnections of two influential contemporary political philosophies with the realist school of thought. Especially in his later writings, Reinhold Niebuhr grappled with the relationships of liberalism and communism with political realism. Chapter III provides as well the intellectual setting for a revisiting of questions raised under the heading of ethics in the context of political philosophy. The issues here concern how political philosophy, existing in the realm of ends, can interact with practical realism, which is operative in the realm of means. Buttressing this mirror-image analysis of realism and certain political philosophies are the contributions of Sir Herbert Butterfield, John Courtney Murray, and Martin Wight.

Chapter IV throws the spotlight on key issues unresolved among major schools of thought. It contrasts systematic thinking, epitomized by the thinkers examined to this point, and systemic theory, illustrated particularly in the work of Kenneth Waltz. Traditionalists write of structures and neorealists of the system. Contemporary approaches in international-relations theory can be likened to a drama in four acts, each act taking the form of a great debate. The first debate occurred in the 1950s and 1960s between realists and idealists. The two protagonists were Columbia University historian Frank Tannenbaum, who saw the debate as a clash between American exceptionalism—we were unique among nation-states—and Hans J. Morgenthau, who was demonized as the father of the evil balance of power doctrine in the United States. The second debate involved the classical versus the scientific approach. Those favoring the scientific approach held out the promise of precise analysis and predictability, whereas the classical thinkers harked back to two thousand years of political thought and emphasized virtue and wisdom. The third debate pitted the authors of the idea of an increasingly interdependent world against those who argued that the nation-state remained the primary actor in international affairs. The fourth debate continues and finds the authors of systemic theory contending with those in the traditional school, who strive for more rigorous and systematic analysis. The issues that divide the various schools of thought remain unresolved. The final debate persists between two groups that identify their views with realism but utilize significantly different concepts and systems.

In the concluding chapter, the discussion returns to realism and idealism and to the growing cynicism toward government and international relations. Disillusionment and distrust have become the disease of the 1990s. Under this broad caption, we search for lessons that will help us understand and possibly combat the public distrust of politicians and public affairs. Watergate, television, and the United Nations have all contributed to spreading the shadow of disillusionment. We seek a way out. Perhaps a more realistic understanding of ourselves and of the world as it is can help point the way. Nothing less than the high stakes of human survival are in the balance.

I

SCHOOLS OF THOUGHT

It has been commonplace in Western Europe to identify fields of study by what are known as schools—the Frankfurt School, the Heidelberg School, the Cologne School, the Munich School. This form of identification has in many ways been alien to American higher education. We tend to look more at universities as represented by certain fields of interest; they stand out because leading American and sometimes European thinkers are in residence doing the teaching and providing the leadership. Thus Christian realism is identified with Reinhold Niebuhr—not with the institution (Union Theological Seminary in New York) at which he taught but with Niebuhr's political and normative thought. There may be some merit in our approach. Ours may be an example of the primacy of the individual in American thought.

In recent years, however, to carry the thought a bit further, some observers have called attention to the fact that in the founding of the study of international relations, certain schools and universities have had a disproportionate influence. That is to say, particular institutions took the lead in a given sphere of scientific or intellectual endeavor in building up a faculty, forming a staff, organizing an extensive library, and transmitting knowledge and evidence of the work being done at their institution.

The focus in this chapter is on three schools of thought and three institutions that are said to have created approaches or perspectives in international relations: the Chicago School, the Yale/Princeton School, and the Harvard School. The reason for discussing these institutions will be obvious to those who have studied or are studying the development of international-relations thinking. To uncover the origins of the field, one has to go back to the 1930s, 1940s, and 1950s. The significance of these decades will be less obvious to some, and for them this inquiry may also help in understanding a more recent period—the 1970s and 1980s. For this reason, it seems entirely justifiable to go back to the roots of the study of international relations and in the process try to place in perspective some of the leading figures at these institutions. For example, at Chicago in the 1940s–1960s, Quincy Wright and Hans J. Morgenthau were the leading scholars of international relations. In the 1940s and 1950s, Yale University conducted a vigorous recruiting program in an effort to match what was going on at Chicago and Harvard. In fact, the leading people at Yale came from institutions such as Chicago but remained to build up strong and significant programs at Yale before transferring virtually en masse to Princeton. At Harvard, William Yandell Elliott, Carl J. Friedrich, Rupert Emerson, and younger scholars were pioneers in developing an approach to international studies grounded in political theory.

THE CHICAGO SCHOOL

The Chicago program merits study because the dominant methodology in international studies on the midway struck roots as much in the study of American government as in international-relations studies. Certain novel analytic approaches to American government were the province of scholars such as Charles Merriam. He joined the department in 1900, became chairman in 1923, and gave up the title—if not the power—in 1940. Merriam insisted that the study of American government had to be based on the study of politics as such. He taught politics to practitioners no less than to theorists. He was active in programs that led to an empirical product, or a product that could serve those in government as well as political theorists and historians. The programs of "the Chief," as he was called, were the creation of a respected thinker who was engaged in the public administration and politics of city government in Chicago. He was also active nationally, for example, in the formation of the President's Committee on Administrative Management. He is described as "the most important social science entrepreneur of his day."[1] He worked closely with colleagues and friends who set up "1313," the Public Administration Clearing House, which brought together many state and local programs in public administration. He was part of an initiative that led eventually to the creation of the National Academy of Public Administration. He was interested in what colleagues across the board were doing to develop the administrative field. They included academic colleagues, like Leonard White and Floyd Reeves, and advisers to government and organizational planners, like Louis Brownlow and Herbert Emmerich. He made it his business to practice politics in the real world, involving himself—at least on a limited scale—in Chicago politics. He was alderman of the fifth ward. He ran for mayor of Chicago and was narrowly defeated. Some say his rival stole the election.

His colleagues called Merriam "the Chief" because of his ability to take charge, and the name was appropriate. He seemed to have the ability, sometimes with limited resources, to attract others who shared his interests. As chairman from 1923 to 1940, he had a hand in the recruitment of rising scholars, including Harold Lasswell, Harold Gosnell, Frederick Schuman, Nathan Leites, Leonard White, and Quincy Wright, all of whom came to Chicago from other institutions. They were to form the Merriam dynasty, which was kept alive by White and Herman Pritchett, White's handpicked successor. Their interest in Merriam's work was an outgrowth of his philosophy that administration separated from politics was unlikely to be a fruitful field of study. Ironically, White, to whom Merriam transferred his power, saw administration as something separate from politics. Lasswell wrote a book defining politics as "who gets what, when, and where." The title was designed to make people reflect that, even within a bureaucracy, the play of politics goes on more or less continuously. One aspect was competition between interest groups; special interests were emerging.

Merriam anticipated certain theories of group politics. He was the author of a book entitled *New Aspects of Politics*. He wrote about political parties and coalition politics even though he opposed any theory of politics based on group interests. New forces were appear-

1. Mark C. Smith, *Social Science in the Crucible: The American Debate over Objectivity and Purpose, 1918–1941* (Durham, 1944), 84.

ing on the scene. Even in his final years, Merriam retained an interest in the new forces of politics and did not exclude them from consideration. He left the psychopathology of politics to Lasswell and an all-out mathematical approach to Gosnell. For him, "The primary goal of politics was to eliminate wasteful activities such as war, revolution, and class and ethnic conflict. 'Improper adjustments' such as these could be eliminated by technical aspects. . . . In Merriam's confident world 'the future is a problem of social engineering.'"[2]

By his example, Merriam must have had a hand in attracting Paul Douglas and Adlai Stevenson to politics. Their activities (Douglas became senator, Stevenson governor) did not go unnoticed by members of the Chicago School. Some who supported them had only marginal connections with the university, but others were full-time faculty members. Douglas was a member of the economics faculty. He sometimes taught principles of economics by passing out handfuls of oranges to hungry consumer-students who, as they consumed, illustrated the law of diminishing returns. Stevenson never performed that way. He was an intellectual, not an actor. Other political figures on the fringes of the Chicago School made unique contributions. A future mayor and fifth-ward alderman named Richard Daley stands out in everyone's memory. We graduate students were able to persuade the mayor and other political figures to participate in university programs, in part because of their contacts with Merriam.

Merriam's interest in the study of American politics and American government reflected an interest in institutions. How does America govern itself? What institutions does a president need? In 1937, the Committee on Administrative Management issued a report entitled "The President Needs Help." That title stemmed from the interest of Merriam and his colleagues in providing institutional backstopping for presidents. They recommended the creation of the Bureau of the Budget and other Executive Office institutions they hoped would both assist the president and perform a coordinating function. They called attention to the need for the establishment of a White House staff to serve the president directly. Before this point, many tasks were farmed out to other departments of government.

So it was Merriam who was the driving force, the center of de-

2. *Ibid.*, 88.

cisions, and the spearhead of action; what an imposing figure he was. Strong and tall with the remains of a great mop of hair, he was a colorful personality who attracted the student body as well as the faculty. For many years he had given a Wednesday evening seminar that was required for all graduate students. By the time some of us appeared on the scene after the war, he had reached retirement. Thus any history of the Chicago School must begin with a discussion of someone who, as a contributor to that school, was not even an international-relations scholar. When Merriam passed on, his son Robert continued certain limited aspects of his work. The younger Merriam was primarily interested in local government, the Congress, and the political process, not directly in international relations. He was more a practitioner than a scholar, although he did attend meetings of the American Political Science Association. By contrast, some of the interpreters who came to Chicago and then went elsewhere were genuinely interested in the realities of international relations.

Harold Lasswell has already been mentioned. Lasswell introduced into the study of law and politics—particularly when he migrated to Yale but even at Chicago—the study of political, social, and psychological forces and their influence on the law. He drew on other social scientists. He was imposing by any standard. At the end of his master's degree exam, he was invited to leave the office while the committee deliberated his fate. Rumor has it that Leonard White, the chairman of his committee, turned to Quincy Wright on the committee and said, "I assume, gentlemen, that the question is not whether Mr. Lasswell has passed but how we can keep him from coming back for his Ph.D. and making an even worse fool of us all."

Lasswell's impact cannot be overestimated, even though his successors in the Chicago School took a different slant on the study of politics and international relations. He was extremely active in national societies. He was president of most of the professional associations. He was at the center of all the debates about the direction of the profession that took place in the American Political Science Association. He was an antagonist, willing and able to hold his own; he was seized with the need to create more scientific rigor in the study of politics. Others had reservations about this approach, but Lasswell was unyielding in asserting that science and psychology were the great hope for the evolution of political science. The future of the study of politics was in becoming a science and not simply a collection of opinions.

Nathan Leites was a close personal friend and disciple of Lasswell. He had an interest in Communist states and wrote about the Politburo's operational code. The operational code was the process by which Communist regimes gained and kept power, ruled, and took advantage of the functions of the Communist party. There were others. Some were younger and several were in other departments. Walter Johnson was an American historian with a lively interest in American politics. Johnson was Adlai Stevenson's biographer and a friend and protégé of Charles Merriam, with a penchant for action. Whenever Merriam lectured or appeared anywhere, Johnson was likely to be in the entourage. He collected writings about politicians, aphorisms, and anecdotes. He and others saw Merriam as a role model and an inspiration. One can trace Merriam's influence across a broad range of political thinking at Chicago.

The reason that Merriam and his friends are important for international studies at the Chicago School is because they influenced the leadership in the international-relations program. Merriam, Johnson, and Lasswell in particular supported and influenced the core group in international relations to explore new and important theories. For instance, in reading *The Study of War* or *The Study of International Relations* by Quincy Wright, one finds that others had planted ideas that Wright and his colleagues later took up as a subject for study.

The founder of the Chicago School and of international studies was Quincy Wright. Throughout his career, he continued to write and think about international-relations programs. He came to Chicago in 1931 and was then in his early forties. Immediately, he began teaching courses in international law, usually divided into two one-semester courses. One was the International Law of Peace and the other the International Law of War. The two courses became legendary at Chicago. They were based on the case-method approach to international law. Wright's encyclopedic interests pushed him in the direction of new ways of thinking and new approaches, and Lasswell always had some novel concept or fresh approach to offer. There were also historians who, from the beginning, had an interest in the Chicago School of international relations. As a footnote, it is noteworthy that, despite Lasswell and others, the Chicago School—in contrast to Yale—never moved too far from its core interest in institutions, history, and processes. The history of international relations going back to World War I was a subject worthy of Quincy Wright's attention. William Halperin, Louis Gottschalk, and European refugee scholars made up part of the international-relations school at Chicago, and influences such as theirs were to continue throughout the life of the school.

Among the economists who had interests in the international relations program were Lloyd Metzler, Bert Hoselitz, and Theodore W. Schultz. Hoselitz was an economic-development authority who founded a unique journal in development studies that emphasized the importance of culture. Various scholars doing more conventional research in economics rounded out this segment of international relations. It proved awkward to fit economics into the traditional international-relations curriculum. Economists argue that students of international relations need to study the basics of economics, including economic theory, to understand the field and say anything worthwhile. Although students recognize that theory and econometrics are important and strengthen their qualifications, such requirements have often kept many international-relations students from taking economics. With a program of requirements as demanding as Chicago's, it was difficult enough to fit all the other disciplines into the program. The core requirements were international law, international politics, international history, and international sociology.

Quincy Wright was convinced that such a program provided the best framework for international studies. He also undertook to create, for the first time at Chicago, an interdisciplinary committee on international relations. It was not a discipline in the usual sense. It did not provide the same in-depth study in a single discipline that economics or government departments offered, but it soon became a vital, active, and prestigious program. It offered students an opportunity to take nine or ten required courses in a broad area of international relations. At some point, students chose an area for specialization. The group who were among the earliest postwar students of the committee in the 1950s and 1960s almost all received appointments in government, business, and banking because of the breadth and intensity of the program. Here was an effort to train people in international relations as such, rather than simply add to the existing courses of political science something on international law or history or whatever the subject might be.

The Committee on International Relations and the Department of Political Science also gave students considerable flexibility to take courses outside their department. For instance, I took the early and middle period in American history as my so-called related field of interest to supplement my work in international studies. I was always glad that I did, because I received preparation that enabled me to locate events, institutions, and leaders who took part in the political history and process of government of the United States. In other words, I could better understand Lincoln's attitude toward other countries because I understood something about his historical period, and the same for Woodrow Wilson's leadership during and after World War I. My understanding of international relations was enhanced by a grounding in history.

All this was facilitated because interdisciplinary work was encouraged, certainly by the Committee on International Relations but also by the Department of Political Science. The course requirements for the committee and the department were different, and that had an impact. It was assumed that anybody getting a Ph.D. in international relations in the government department should know a lot about constitutional law, political parties, public administration, political theory, and so on. That made for excellent preparation for teaching. It was also assumed in the Committee on International Relations that a similar emphasis on other related areas of study should be encouraged.

The golden age of the Committee on International Relations at the University of Chicago began with the arrival of Hans J. Morgenthau, not only because of his contribution but equally because of the creative interaction that occurred between the founder of the study of international politics—Morgenthau—and the founder of international law at Chicago—Quincy Wright.

Most graduate students returning from military service in the mid-1940s had heard nothing about Morgenthau. He was a relative unknown. He had taught at Brooklyn College and Kansas City University. He had come to this country without any contacts or a job. Most refugee scholars had friends who looked out for them long before they reached our shores. Morgenthau knew one person on the American university scene—a professor at Columbia University. He tells in his autobiography of climbing the long steps of Low Library and taking the elevator to the professor's office. The person answering the door shook his head and said that the friend had died more than a year before. His one possible contact was no longer alive. In comparison with most German refugee scholars, Morgenthau was all alone.

Later, Morgenthau moved to Chicago as a substitute for Wright while he was at the Nuremberg trials. For students at Chicago, a certain mystique surrounded Wright's public service. Most of us who became part of the Chicago School tended to gravitate initially toward him. Wright was strongly supported by advisers to students, research and teaching assistants, and paper graders—all the activities that make up appointments and financial assistance for graduate students. Not long after I arrived at Chicago, I became Wright's graduate student assistant. I was assigned to grade papers and give exams for him. I helped with some research materials for his articles and books.

Wright inspired the interest of most of us who came to Chicago because of his ongoing involvement in the policymaking process in Washington. He was an adviser to Justice Robert Jackson at the Nuremberg trials. He had a role that excited young, impressionable graduate students, who welcomed having contact with someone who was obviously close to the scene of action. He was also a polite and generous person in most respects. He was genuinely interested in his best students getting involved in programs such as the Chicago Council on Foreign Relations and, even more, the United Nations Association of Chicago, which he and his wife had helped establish. Participation lent a practical aura to our work. The Wrights were not only "people of the library." They were people of action, and this made them stand out among ivory-tower scholars at Chicago.

Wright had several other qualities that intrigued and excited students. He had done studies that involved large-scale research and writing contributions by graduate students. His writings seemed to reflect the real world more than the research of the library scholar seeking to ferret out the facts and the history of a given issue. Wright was also at the center of those who funded programs at Chicago, a group whose leader was Charles Merriam. His most famous research project with student participation was the *Study of War* project, but there were others. He turned to students to help him organize the various Norman Waite Harris conferences funded from the Harris endowment. In almost every respect, his work had merit for students. It appealed to young people. I had applied to Harvard Law School and the Graduate School at the University of Chicago. Since it was late in the day, I made up my mind that whichever reply came first I would accept. The acceptance from Chicago came first. I didn't hesitate a minute. I sent in my registration and acceptance immediately, and the nature of my choice made Wright's approach that much more interesting.

After coming to the University of Chicago, Morgenthau throughout the war was part of a four-man department. He soon became a well-known personality, and myths quickly surrounded him. One was that anybody who wanted to fail an oral examination or have a dissertation rejected should choose Morgenthau as an adviser. He was said to be a tough, relentless, and uncompromising critic. This may have been true with marginal students, but he was always unusually helpful to serious students. Although he may not have particularly enjoyed reading great volumes of student papers, I think he understood why they were an important responsibility, and he graded most of them himself.

Morgenthau had written on various topics in normative theory: norms and politics, norms and reality, and norms and history. He had published scholarly papers and at least one small book in Europe before coming to this country. Students had only a vague sense of his European scholarship. He was also known as a hard taskmaster and Germanic lecturer who entered and left the classroom at precisely the same moment for every class session. He was someone who would not let students get away with haphazard research and writing. He was polite but never got too close to individual students. As the years went by, he became known as a professor who was increasingly receptive to exchanging ideas with graduate students, colleagues, and others. He became more Americanized in the process and more interested and willing to trade gossip and information, including what various people had said about him.

Morgenthau and Wright went their separate ways. Wright was

clearly the leader of the majority group in international studies. Morgenthau just as clearly supervised the work of a growing minority. Without ever seeming to do so, Wright was an extraordinarily effective promoter of his own point of view. He did so through membership—and eventually leadership—in all the professional societies. He regularly attended larger and smaller conferences around the country and was in demand as a consultant to a host of government agencies. Without appearing to push the matter, Wright was effective as a politician within the academic community. Morgenthau not only did not *appear* to push his political interests. In fact, he did not and perhaps could not have done so. At least at first, he saw his contribution as that of the lone scholar pursuing truth, as Goethe said, in a spirit of free inquiry. He put that goal well ahead of all others.

Yet Morgenthau, in spite of his nonpolitical approach and what sometimes seemed shyness and withdrawal, made close friends and gained staunch defenders, particularly among his students. At two extremes on the spectrum, Morgenthau earned significant admiration and support. The one extreme was the group who made up present and former students, some of whom called him Hans. The other extreme was that of a handful of university leaders, most notably President Robert M. Hutchins, who respected his philosophical approach, closely linked with the history of philosophy and political experience in the Western world. Even with Hutchins he had limited contacts, in part because of his candor. Once Hutchins described an idea he had had and explained that his father thought the idea was crazy. Morgenthau responded, "He has a point." That interrupted their relations for years.

It would be a mistake to think that Morgenthau failed to communicate with important persons or that he had no interest in politics or in the profession. In fact, he communicated more or less continuously through more than nine thousand letters and through the interest and response that he showed former students, colleagues, and friends around the country. Both men were in demand at many universities. Their influence was in part a result of the demand for them as visiting lecturers. Wright seemed to focus on what people favored at the time—peace, law, and order. Morgenthau raised questions and spoke primarily of continuity and change in the history of international relations.

If the era of the late 1940s, 1950s, and 1960s was the golden age of the Chicago School, it was in large part because of the presence of Morgenthau and Wright. Their objectives and their thought differed in significant ways. Morgenthau called attention to the need for a political approach to international relations. He put first the understanding of political rivalries and disputes that were forever present, erupting periodically in crises and open conflict. He lectured on power and interests and the balance of power.

Wright was the prophet of international law and organization and a child of science, who saw science as a means of transforming international politics. By contrast, Morgenthau was a lifelong skeptic so far as science and politics were concerned. In his first major work, *Scientific Man Versus Power Politics,* he staked out the broad outlines of his thinking. He argued that because Western societies had elevated science and reason as the main route to peace, they had lost touch with the historic traditions of statecraft. By comparison, Wright was open to the possibility that science might in various important ways lead to the restructuring and reorientation of both theory and practice in international relations. He came from a family of scientists. Morgenthau, on the other hand, linked his approach and his world view to the two-thousand-year history of politics and relations among societies in the Western world. He was as familiar with Aristotle and Plato or Augustine and Aquinas as he was with contemporary writers—perhaps more so.

Wright was not irreconcilably opposed to Morgenthau's emphasis on political theory. Indeed, he had a continuing interest in Hobbes and Locke, Hume and Rousseau. I always thought, however, that Wright's knowledge of political theory was more a product of conversations and snatches of information than of any intensive study of the texts. Never did his interest in political theory match his interest in pursuing new and engaging ways of thinking about international relations, including institution-building and ideas gleaned from colleagues in the biological and physical sciences. Wright was a believer in science almost to the same degree that Morgenthau was an agnostic, skeptical that science could ever change the nature of man or the character of politics among nations. Morgenthau had a European knowledge of history; he had read and assimilated all the classical writings of European philosophers, historians, and statesmen. He emphasized the lessons of history for international politics. Wright was inclined to examine the past for clues or insights that pointed to possible routes to a new and better world.

My observations about Wright and Morgenthau could be expanded indefinitely. The two men were the pivotal and dominant figures at Chicago. They *made* the University of Chicago what it was in the forties and fifties—the leading center of international studies. They drew closer together in the last years of their lives. Neither was afraid to acknowledge the truth in the other's viewpoint. Their references to each other became more frequent and reflected growing respect and a deepening mutual affection.

Nonetheless, to understand the roots of the clash between their contending viewpoints and leadership at the Chicago School, one has to go back to an earlier period, to the dominant figure at Chicago—Charles Merriam. Merriam and Morgenthau were exemplars of two contending philosophical views about politics, its study, reality, and future. Merriam's career is full of ironies. He "was a political theorist who denied the utility of theory, a champion of quantitative social science who could not do the most elementary calculations . . . and strangest of all, a politician who insisted that social scientists must be completely apolitical." He said he believed that "any problem could be solved by relying on intelligence and reasoning capacity." He was hardly the first political scientist to call for a science of politics, but no one ever organized so thorough a campaign to promote it. The formation of Merriam's approach to politics went back at least to 1915, when he was active in Chicago politics. Merriam was a midwesterner who brought a spirit of optimism and enthusiasm to Chicago. His view of political science was predicated on the view that political science, through new scientific and administrative techniques, could bring about patterns of change that would improve politics and society. He had an observer's interest in social-science theory and concepts but little scientific competence or know-how. Although he collaborated with Harold Gosnell on a statistical analysis of nonvoting, he did little of the quantitative work and, according to Gosnell, "understood even less of it." Yet his admiration of statistics came from "his intense belief in the supremacy of science and the scientific method."[3]

3. *Ibid.*, 84, 87, 88, 90, 92–93.

Merriam often said that instead of going back to Aristotle to examine forms of government, scholars should make a list of eight or ten different types of regimes—federalism, democracy, republicanism, and so on—and study these instead. Progress and reform were two of the qualities that Charles Merriam brought to the Chicago legacy, and that spirit was to live on for decades after he was gone. It was represented by people who held quite different points of view. For Merriam, unquestioned progress was something that should be taken as a given, not something to be proven or disproven. Progress involved dynamic efforts by strong leaders and brave warriors defending the truth. He saw the role of political scientists as that of foot soldiers fighting to sustain a philosophy of progress and reform but within a scientific and objective mode. Thus for him, science and progress were joined.

Furthermore, Merriam linked his optimism with a second outlook—the philosophy of science. He went back to Walter Bagehot in seeking inspiration for some of his putative political theory. He drew on the work that Bagehot had begun in his study of constitutions and politics. Merriam believed that science had not moved ahead in the study of politics because scholars had not been active and vigorous enough in promoting and practicing it. Don Price has shown that American political science sought to substitute science and administration for politics.[4] An act of will could ensure that science and public administration would change and improve politics.

However strongly held his view of science and progress, Merriam went about his own work. He was the most successful spokesman for the social sciences in the country. He was also a consummate fundraiser. He liked to raise questions and pose issues rather than offer definitive answers. Yet there is no question that he expressed enthusiasm for the influence of science on the theory and practice of government and politics—a view that later generations were to question and criticize. He was ever vigilant in examining the credentials of those who sought appointments at Chicago. His goal, whether fully conscious or not, was to recruit scholars like Quincy Wright, Leonard White, and Harold Lasswell who, above all, must be sympathetic to science. In his study of politics, if not in occupying his

4. Don K. Price, *America's Unwritten Constitution: Science, Religion, and Political Responsibility* (Baton Rouge, 1983).

chair, Lasswell succeeded Merriam in the government department at Chicago. In other words, Merriam introduced his own preferences in the selection of the faculty and the shaping of the department. He was a powerful force at Chicago and across the nation, and he sought to gain and hold power. It was inevitable he would oppose another leader who was criticizing the icon of science that Merriam had embraced.

All this being true, no one should have been surprised when Merriam attacked Morgenthau for *Scientific Man*. The book criticized the view of society and politics that saw science and reason as transforming agents of politics and a substitute for statesmanship. Merriam, who knew how to exercise power, went into battle even though he had prophesied the end of conflict in society. He went so far as to suggest that Morgenthau's philosophy was not appropriate at Chicago. When Morgenthau published *Scientific Man,* Merriam made known his displeasure. He suggested to Morgenthau that he might, as a lawyer and European scholar, teach courses on administrative law. This putdown followed logically because Merriam was convinced that just as physics and chemistry had become a science, efforts to introduce a scientific approach into the study of politics merited support. Science could remove the contingencies and accidents that had limited politics in the past. In sum, Merriam's influence and power at Chicago were enormous, and he chose to use his power against Chicago's greatest critic of science.

Long after Merriam was gone, his view of the study of politics lived on in the work of such other political scientists as David Easton and Avery Leiserson and, indirectly, Herman Pritchett and Quincy Wright. It was a viewpoint and approach to the study of politics that was to become a dominant form of thinking, whoever its spokesmen. Morgenthau was, however, equally forceful and determined in pushing the opposite point of view. One way to describe their differences is to say that, on almost every issue of methodology and political philosophy, the opposite of Merriam's formulation describes Morgenthau. Indeed, Morgenthau insisted that we had been pursuing in politics and society a false view that saw human beings as readily susceptible to manipulation and control—social engineering. This view underestimated what was unique about individual human beings. It had little to say about statecraft. It looked on society as a kind of laboratory for social and political experimentation. It accepted political manipulation and social engineering as the main route to change. Looking ahead, Merriam was optimistic; looking back, at past experience, Morgenthau suspended judgment on the future but was anxious. In some areas, however, he was hopeful. For instance, he argued for our ability to deal with the Soviet Union through diplomacy long before the fall of our adversary. He was a believer in democracy but pessimistic in other areas. For example, he saw continuing challenges in the relationship between individuals and society.

Morgenthau did not so much oppose the kind of work that Merriam outlined; rather, he questioned whether prophecies of its triumph were justified by history or by the progress that had been made through science up to the present. In other words, if science had the ability to change and transform man and society, why had it not done so in the centuries from the Enlightenment to the present? Were the stubborn and intractable qualities of human nature obstacles to the achievement of any natural harmony of interests patterned on the harmonies of the universe? Did they provide a true reading of the political universe? Why was rivalry and the contest for power between people and groups in society so persistent if a little more science and a little more reason in human relations could change all that? In proclaiming his views, Morgenthau challenged the most powerful political scientist at Chicago. He attacked the most popular approach to politics of the time. For that, Merriam and his followers never forgave him.

Morgenthau carried on his crusade with support from abroad, including scholars in England. With his publications came the kind of recognition that comes to anyone who has taken a strong position and defends it, whether or not everyone agrees with him. He made his way slowly but surely from the point where he had been so savagely attacked and challenged by Merriam, who suggested he should drop the work he had undertaken in philosophy, science, and politics. Morgenthau's critique of science and social reform was hard medicine for those who thought that a few more methodologies and concepts or economic innovations would transform society and the nature of political relationships.

A great deal more study and thought could be given to the relationship between these two powerful figures. Suffice it to say it is more illuminating to look at Morgenthau in this context than to study him in isolation or to retrace the various stages in his relations with Quincy Wright, with whom he could disagree but with whom he also shared a fairly broad area of common interest. (As is often true, it was the *followers* of each of the two giants who most often exaggerated the differences between the two men and did so for their own purposes.) It was Merriam more than Wright who believed that science would save society and insisted there were multiple paths to this end, including public administration.

"The Chief" was untiring in organizing the Social Science Research Council, funding the construction of a social-science building at the university, and bringing together the constituent groups at Chicago's 1313 and the Public Administration Clearing House. He and Brownlow worked out of a suite in the Hay-Adams Hotel in Washington and through myriad organizations in the capital, all of which were potential missionaries for extending his view of society. Merriam was always successful in obtaining resources. He had strong allies that included members of the President's Committee on Administration Management. He was a popular figure and knew what it meant to take care of a payroll in politics. He also knew what it meant to lose, having been defeated in several political ventures. Even after his defeat, he was appointed an adviser to the Chicago city government. Until the end of his life, calls came regularly from Washington, New York, and from abroad. The advantage Merriam had was that, whereas Morgenthau was a theorist, it was assumed that Merriam knew politics and what he was talking about because in fact he had been deeply involved in social-science politics and in local and national politics.

More study is needed on the possible interconnections and the compatibility or incompatibility of these two remarkable figures and their distinctive points of view. Popular interest in Morgenthau's writings tends to give recognition to his contribution in international politics, but no less central is his view of politics and political theory. His view of politics provided a more comprehensive theory than Merriam's because it went back to the classical and Christian view of the nature of man and the nature of politics. To this day, the debate continues concerning the two philosophies, and the same arguments are often used. The differences between the two major figures and their philosophies will almost certainly persist far into the future.

THE HARVARD SCHOOL

Oftentimes, discussions of Harvard's standing, whatever the field, begin with the proposition that "Harvard is Harvard." Its history and traditions, outstanding students, well-known faculty, and mystique virtually guarantee its prestige across the country. Yet there are exceptions, as with departments that rise and fall in national rankings and a certain dispersion of effort as prominent professors depart periodically to become public officials or consultants in government or accept joint faculty appointments here and abroad. After World War II, Carl J. Friedrich and Karl Deutsch spent up to half of each year at institutions abroad, such as the University of Heidelberg or the University of Frankfurt. Name droppers who follow the staffing of each new administration in Washington invariably point to the presence of Harvard personalities scattered liberally throughout the new governments.

The emphasis at Harvard in the 1930s and 1940s was international law, with George Grafton Wilson in the government department and Manley Hudson in the Law School. On the various projects to strengthen international law or codify and formulate it in statements and texts, Wilson and Hudson were almost always at or near the center of events. Other text writers, such as Charles Cheney Hyde and Clarence Berdahl, found homes in the Midwest, the Northeast, the West Coast, and the South.

By the mid-1940s, international law at Harvard was on the decline. Payson Wild taught a course or two, but he was destined to become a Harvard dean and then provost at Northwestern. (He was nominated for president at Northwestern, but for political reasons, the dean of the Medical School, "Rocky" Miller, was tapped.) Payson Wild was a charming and gracious man who may have been too even-handed and eclectic to replace the colorful Wilson. Nevertheless, he was a friend and source of inspiration to younger colleagues at Northwestern, of whom I was one. One observer notes of Wild: "He was not a specialist of Wilson's weight." To that I would add, "He chose rather to be an educational leader." Four other scholars undertook to preserve the tradition. They were Hans Kelsen, Inis Claude, Louis Sohn, and Leo Gross. Kelsen was a visiting professor who migrated to Berkeley; Claude was a young assistant professor destined for leadership elsewhere; Sohn taught in the Law School; and Leo Gross joined the Harvard faculty, mainly in the summers, while holding a permanent professorship at the Fletcher School of Law and Diplomacy. My colleague I. L. Claude wrote his master's thesis with Gross on the design of the U.N. specialized agencies and went on to become a distinguished authority on international institutions and international relations and to teach at the Universities of Michigan and Virginia. I have learned most of what I know about Harvard from him.

By 1946, political theory had supplanted international law as the dominant field in Harvard's government department. It was the cornerstone of the discipline, and Friedrich's full-year course—the history of political philosophy—was required of every graduate student. Indeed, the hallmark of Harvard Ph.D.'s in government was solid grounding in political theory. Harvard's famous Government I course was half political theory; the rest was American government, comparative government, and a smattering of international relations. The goal in the Ph.D. program was the training of generalists, starting with political theory plus three other subfields, each divided into two sectors. (For example, the international field included comparative government and international relations.) Two areas of study in other departments, such as history and economics, met the outside field requirements. Graduate students who pursued the program earned credentials as political scientists with specialization in a subfield such as international relations. If philosophy earlier was the queen of the sciences, political theory was at the heart of political science at Harvard, setting it apart from Chicago and Yale at the time.

In the period under discussion, an interest in public policy made its appearance at Harvard, primarily in the Littauer School but also in the government department. Military service by faculty members in World War II was a factor that inspired the movement but so was participation in the founding of the United Nations at San Francisco. Rupert Emerson with Ralph Bunche had been involved in the administration of certain U.S. dependencies. Economists such as Ed Mason and Max Millikan (of MIT) had learned to cooperate with both private and public agencies. (While working at the Rockefeller Foundation, I was impressed by the efficiency with which both men replied to inquiries.) McGeorge Bundy had a window on government as a participant-observer writing on Henry Stimson. William Yandell Elliott, whose book *The Pragmatic Revolt* was a minor classic, abandoned his primary interest in political theory and commuted to Capitol Hill. He imported public figures to meet with his students, and he founded Harvard's international seminars later handed over to his protégé, Henry Kissinger. The seminars enabled Kissinger to make contact with high-level foreign leaders, with some of whom he was to work as secretary of state. Taken together, these separate initiatives set in motion future public-policy programs that spread across departments at Harvard.

Insofar as specific international-relations professors and their subjects were concerned, Harvard's foremost strength was in its breadth of coverage more than in the presence of intellectual giants of the stature of Wright, Morgenthau, or Wolfers at Yale. Friedrich was the exception, but his interests were more in constitutionalism and theory. If there were scholars of such dimensions they came later. I knew Rupert Emerson and traveled with him in Africa. He was a gentle and friendly senior professor who never succumbed to the disease of Harvarditis. He invited some of us to make presentations at Harvard and contributed to the development of some of the country's early Africanists, namely James Coleman and Martin Kilson. Yet Emerson came to the study and teaching of Africa somewhat late in his career. His main interests had been nationalism, imperialism, and international organization. Merle Fainsod, who was a vital and energetic scholar, collaborated with Lincoln Gordon on a text in administrative regulation and became a leading student of Soviet affairs. In addition to international law, Payson Wild introduced a course on American foreign policy that Bundy took over on Wild's departure. When he was in Cambridge, Elliott combined offerings in U.S. foreign policy and British Commonwealth politics with his first love—political theory. Early in his career, Elliott gave every sign of becoming an intellectual giant, but he chose rather to become a public figure and eventually took up a post-retirement position at American University in Washington. Bruce Hopper taught some international politics courses but, in the words of one of his colleagues, was largely "sidelined" and ignored by the department. William T. R. Fox (who taught at all three institutions) and Charles Michaud were visiting professors during the summer, and Leo Gross was a frequent visitor.

Area studies—except for those on the Soviet area—were non-existent, and the development of area expertise was a task individual scholars were expected to pursue on their own. Yale had a larger stable of luminaries in international relations than Harvard. By contrast, Chicago was the home of a pair of scholars who largely set the framework for the great debates in international relations, perhaps for generations to come.

To Harvard's advantage, it was the hub of the international-relations network in Cambridge, Boston, and, to some extent, the rest of the world. It drew on Fletcher (Gross, and before he moved to Harvard, Deutsch), MIT (Norman Padelford, Max Millikan, Paul Samuelson, and Walt Rostow), and Brandeis, to mention only three institutions. There were Boston University, Boston College, Tufts, and others. The Law School Forum and other lecture series brought significant speakers from all over the world. The World Peace Foundation was the publisher of *International Organization*. Claude, Emerson, Gross, Wright, and I served on its editorial board. It also had a superb library at which Claude and colleagues did research for their doctoral dissertations and other writings. Its board meetings dealt with substance and were marked by intense discussion of prospective articles and the core issues for international organizations. Board members considered the process the most rigorous they had experienced in serving on editorial boards.

What can be said about Harvard's place in the development of international relations? How did it compare with Yale and Chicago? Because it was Harvard and could boast outstanding students and faculty, it clearly was one of the early "Big Three." The breadth of its coverage of international relations exceeded Chicago's. Because the majority of the researchers at what was called the "Dunn Center" (its director was Frederick S. Dunn) did little teaching, it had a smaller number of active professors than Harvard, even though the number of luminaries at the center and in the department at Yale may have been greater. When one looks back, however, on the intellectual strengths at the three institutions and asks whose writings and theories continue to inspire discussion and debate, no one can match Morgenthau and Wright. More student papers, theses, and dissertations are still being written on the theories and concepts of the two Chicago professors than on those of anyone at either Yale or Harvard, with the possible exception of Lasswell. Yet Harvard produced international-relations scholars with an impressive grounding in political theory, and Harvard graduates and their students are active participants and policy advisers in the current debates. Yale has to its credit an array of Ph.D.'s in international relations who compare favorably both in quantity and in quality with the best of Harvard and Chicago. With the passage of time, the apparent monopoly of leadership held by the three in international relations disappeared, and today, alongside the three are centers of excellence at outstanding universities across the country.

THE YALE/PRINCETON SCHOOL

The dominance of Harvard and Chicago in the international-relations field was bound to have a beginning and an end. No institution in a vast and sprawling country such as the United States could for long be the preeminent center when other programs were beginning to take hold. The emergence of the Yale program is an example of the growing decentralization of international-relations studies that has gone on for the last seventy-five years. It also marks the rise of a program that was soon the equal of Chicago's and Harvard's. Their programs went back to a prewar emphasis on diplomatic history, international law, and international organization, with such famous names as Samuel Flagg Bemiss, Edwin Borchard, and Walter Sharp. Even in these fields, however, the Yale approach was distinctive. Nicholas Spykman, who along with Morgenthau was one of the two most conspicuous dissenters at many interwar international law conferences, wrote about the sociological foundations of international politics and international law. His background included the writing of a dissertation on the sociologist Georg Simmel, and his outlook and viewpoint reflected that approach. He based his analysis on sociology and geography and the development of a geostrategic outlook.

Yale had a number of advantages for such a program. One that turned in on itself after a time was the attitude of the president of the university, Whitney Griswold. Griswold was one of America's foremost scholars in Far Eastern history. Some critics, such as John K. Fairbanks, charged he had favored Japan over China in the conflicts of the 1930s. Griswold favored international relations provided that it had a strong historical orientation. This was possible only when the main group of scholars at an institution shared the viewpoint of international history. In the beginning at Yale, the leadership came from Spykman. During this period, Griswold was an effective spokesman with foundations.

Nick Spykman was a fascinating and colorful personality, beloved by colleagues. He died at an early age, cutting short what might have been a more voluminous scholarly output. He signaled to the rest of the country that Yale was a university to reckon with in the fields of international history and international relations. He wrote articles for popular magazines such as *Life,* a major study entitled *America's Strategy in World Politics,* and a more specialized work, *The Geography of the Peace.* In all his writings he sought to broaden the discipline and to call attention to valuable new insights that he felt were on the horizon or were awaiting further development.

The background of the leadership at Yale went beyond Spykman. He had a hand in early recruitment at Yale, but when he died in 1943, his work was continued by the Sterling Professor of International Relations, Arnold Wolfers. Wolfers was born and buried in St. Gallen, Switzerland. He was extremely well liked by his students, and his orientation was well received by almost all his colleagues in the early phase of the Yale program. He was not alone in the program, however. In his own work he continued to emphasize political and diplomatic history. His would-be successors included scholars who had been recruited from around the country. They were to become a major source of Yale's strength in the field but also a problem for the future.

The newcomers to Yale came in considerable numbers from the University of Chicago. William T. R. Fox was one; he had received his Ph.D. degree from and taught courses at Chicago, where both he and his wife, Annette Baker Fox, were highly regarded. But as is often true of rising scholars at educational institutions, he saw greener fields and greater opportunities for advancement at another institution, Yale. His important book on the superpowers, delineating the beginnings of their struggle in the Cold War, represents the more traditional side of his work. At Yale, where he remained for some time, and later at Columbia, Fox turned his attention to more theoretical national-security studies, including a study of NATO.

In the days of Chicago's preeminence as the major school in international relations, Fox would have remained a professor at that institution. Yet he illustrates the migration of some of the ablest people who began at Chicago. With the inauguration of new programs, what was bound to happen occurred first with Fox and the international economist Klaus Knorr. Knorr was a figure of prominence in the overall field of international economics. He introduced young scholars to the international-relations subfield of political economy and became the editor of the influential journal *World Politics.* He was active, even aggressive, in pursuing his own contacts with the U.S. Foreign Service, the State Department, and international financial institutions. In an earlier day, when Chicago was a standout in international relations along with Harvard, he too would probably have remained in the Midwest. Bernard Brodie, author of *The Absolute Weapon,* was another outstanding scholar who migrated from Chicago to Yale and then to Stanford. Some consider him the father of national-security studies in America.

Taking over from Spykman was Frederick S. Dunn, whose research included an important book, *Peaceful Change,* and a definitive study of the Japanese peace treaty. He continued as the administrative head when the center moved to Princeton. He had access to all the diplomatic documents on the treaty. His close ties with prominent Japanophiles like John D. Rockefeller III, who was a consultant to Secretary of State John Foster Dulles in the treaty process, facilitated access to most of the principals in the negotiations and the signing of the Japanese peace treaty. His health declined after the move to Princeton, and Knorr and others increasingly assumed responsibility.

And so it went. A movement from the Midwest to the East had its origins with the Yale Center. Yale and then Princeton faculty have contributed to the proliferation of important centers of international relations across the country. No longer can one point to a few places as being the major centers, even though universities such as Berkeley, Stanford, Columbia, MIT, and Michigan have had outstanding programs. The fact is that mobility within American society and the determination of American scholars to make their mark have led to continuing migration from the Midwest and the East to other parts of the country and to centers around the nation. Significantly, after World War II the Midwest was the hub, others the periphery.

Beginning in the late 1950s, the program at Yale, which was founded by Spykman and carried forward at the teaching level by Arnold Wolfers and newly arrived colleagues from the Midwest and other parts of the country, came on hard times. As a respected historian, Whitney Griswold was a man of strong passions and convictions. He had his own views about how to study international relations and foreign policy. He took offense at some of the more abstract theoretical work that was being introduced at the Yale Center. He also was upset that the new people made independent approaches to funding agencies without his knowledge. He had found it easy to tolerate and respect Spykman and Wolfers, but as time went on and as the more aggressive behaviorist-oriented program at Yale expanded, particularly through the dynamic leadership of some of the new people who moved to Yale, Griswold turned against it.

Along the way, other leading scholars migrated to Yale and in particular the Law School, notably Harold Lasswell and Myres MacDougal. Lasswell was well on the road to developing his own version of analytic theory at Chicago, and he continued such interests as a leading scholar at Yale until his death. Griswold soon made it clear that he would be glad to get rid of the Yale Center and that he would like to see its members go elsewhere. His natural inclination was heightened by certain personal conflicts that arose. Some members of the center chose not to teach or were not invited to teach. Griswold was determined that "the Dunn Center" should not take the place of the more traditional work in history, political science, and sociology. He also thought that the nonteaching research scholars were a luxury Yale could ill afford. So an irreconcilable conflict arose between the president of the university, Whitney Griswold, and the members of the Yale Center. Exactly when contacts with Princeton were made is not clear, but it soon became evident that if Yale was not anxious to continue the Dunn Center, Princeton was.

The entire center and its staff, with the exception of Wolfers, picked up books, computers, and research material and moved en masse to Princeton, where they founded a new center of international affairs. Ted Dunn continued to be the administrative leader, but he was to be succeeded in a relatively short time by Klaus Knorr. This group was a powerhouse in pursuit of its aims and in every other respect. They made it one of their prime objectives to build *World Politics* into what they advertised as the leading journal in international politics and diplomacy. They attracted fellowship money from some of the main sources of support that had traditionally helped Princeton, including the Rockefeller family. Others were interested in the continuation of the work that had started at Yale. They received the full support of the Princeton university administration and became ever stronger as time passed.

At Yale, Arnold Wolfers patiently and skillfully continued his teaching and research before eventually moving on to the School for Advanced International Studies, where he joined Paul H. Nitze as the head of a new foreign-policy institute. Before that, he was a magnet for students who came to Yale from around the country. Indeed, it could be said that the remaining Yale program, perhaps as much as any other, was uniquely successful in attracting some of the best graduate students in the country. Future leaders such as Harold Jacobson, Howard Wriggins, Lucien Pye, Roger Hilsman, and the late Robert Good were part of an assemblage of eight or ten outstanding young people who had their training in the Yale program, primarily with Arnold Wolfers. Their loyalty to him is reflected in the Festschrift they prepared in his honor. Their careers are testimony to his teaching.

Thus the Yale program continued as a fairly traditional international-studies program without hostility to any of the newer approaches. In fact, the good students who had matriculated at Yale frequently chose it over some of the newer programs. It was significant that Yale remained strong after the departure of the entire Yale Center to Princeton University. In effect, what happened with the movement of scholars from Chicago to Yale simply continued in the migration of a comparable group—and, in some cases, an identical group—from Yale to Princeton and other institutions.

This basically can be said to be the history of international studies in the postwar period. Later, other universities became thriving centers for international studies. Scholars owe their primary allegiance to the furtherance of their careers and to the discipline of which they are a part rather than to any single institution. If loyalty to a single institution was strong, it hardly proved a deterrent to professional advancement. What began at Chicago and Harvard was carried on at other leading centers. Professional mobility represents a trend traceable throughout American higher education and continues to the present. No single program in any scholarly field is guaranteed a permanent hold on leadership in any discipline. This has been true of Harvard and of programs and institutions with large endowments no less than of pioneering institutions such as the University of Chicago, established with Rockefeller family contributions and sustained through broad-based funding as the leading university in the Midwest.

Although movement from single institutions seems unfortunate for the institutions concerned, is it not also true that placement of leading people around the country has been beneficial for aspiring graduate students seeking to carve out a career for themselves in international relations? The work that began at institutions like Chicago, Harvard, and Yale has continued. No one could wish to suggest that the three schools have been anything but exemplary leaders in the profession. But at the same time, important as Bruce Russett and Gaddis Smith have been at Yale, or John Mearsheimer and Stephen Walt at Chicago, or Stanley Hoffmann, Joseph Nye, and Samuel Huntington at Harvard, or Robert Gilpin, Henry Bienen, and Richard Falk at Princeton, it can hardly be said that any one institution today or at any time in the foreseeable future can claim dominance over the whole of international relations or of the other disciplines.

What began as a personal perspective on Chicago, Harvard, and Yale, calling attention to the institutional and human resources that these universities enjoyed for the development of international relations (and sometimes the transfer of those institutional resources, as between Yale and Princeton), the picture today is one in which universities and centers in other parts of the country are coming forward with major programs. They offer new visions of international studies or assurances of the continuation of fundamental work that has already begun. They become the newest leading programs. Twenty-five years ago, who would have thought that the University of South Carolina would commit major resources for a new program? Yet under the leadership of Donald Puchala, Betty Glad, and Charles Kegley, among others, the program has flourished, with younger talent and long-term leadership helping it to make its mark.

The debate over the proper focus of international studies will go on for decades to come. Should the emphasis be upon a multi-disciplinary approach or upon fundamental work in one of the basic disciplines, such as political science or history? That issue will pre-occupy the profession in one form or another far into the future. What should be the focus—problem, policy, or theory? Should stud-ies aim to create order out of chaos and bring together in more organized forms, susceptible to evaluation and analysis, the factors that constitute the main elements of international relations? Or should the focus be to develop entirely novel viewpoints? Or to com-bine the old and the new in different theoretical structures?

Early consensus seems unlikely between those in emerging pro-grams and those who have preceded them. The absence of consensus ought not to frighten or disturb leaders in the profession. The fact that new and significant work is undertaken in addition to traditional, time-tested inquiry is a mark of the vitality of the field. If only one viewpoint or one attitude or one concept was given consideration, the field would be stagnant. What is exciting is the number of stu-dents who continue to choose to study international studies at cen-ters such as the one with which I have been associated for almost two decades—the University of Virginia—as well as at other institutions around the country. Many go on to teaching opportunities or lead-ership in education as a whole. Others continue with foreign-service appointments or work in international business, banking, and fi-nance. The broad base of studies that they have pursued in international-relations centers is a source of strength in their career development and in the furtherance of the field. So what is seen in some places as the decline of international studies can be seen overall as its strengthening and the broadening of vistas for the years ahead. That, it seems to me, is a substantial asset for international studies, however much some of us go back to Chicago, Harvard, and Yale. In the last forty years the study of international relations has become a national enterprise from which, it can be hoped, society will benefit well into the twenty-first century.

I hesitate to qualify this positive and blissful picture, but I see an ominous and threatening shadow that has appeared only in the last five years. It is the growing tendency to adopt one approach because it reflects the dominant view of a majority in the professional societies. Departments and bureaucracies are becoming obsessed with national ratings, and a professional elite, because of its resources, claims the right to judge. Yet those who seek position and power in professional bureaucracies are seldom intellectual leaders engaged in the search for truth. More often they expend their energy in bureaucratic politics. They occupy the stage for a brief moment and are replaced by new seekers of influence and power. To make them the arbiters of professional evaluations is to substitute politics for educational growth and development. A host of factors was responsible for the emergence of Chicago, Harvard, and Yale in international studies, but concern for ratings was secondary. Except for Wright and Lasswell, the early giants in international studies were not much concerned with professional societies and ratings. The current preoccupation with ratings will pass.

II

INTEREST AND ETHICS:
THEORY AND PRACTICE

REINHOLD NIEBUHR

Schools of thought are the product less of highly ranked institutions, more often of powerful individuals who have shaped the main currents of thought. Among the political and normative theorists, Reinhold Niebuhr is for many the preeminent figure. Three factors—Niebuhr's personality, his works, and the spirit of his times—are inseparable to an understanding of his influence on religious and political thought. He appeared at a time when confusion abounded about the possibility of a viable economy, the dual threat of fascism and communism in the world, the role of education, and the unprecedented rise of the United States to world leadership, seemingly overnight. The United States had been isolationist and an unknown factor in the balance of power in Europe and the rest of the world. Yet in World War II, America emerged as the decisive element in determining victory or defeat, and it has continued to play this role in the postwar world.

Hitler had predicted that the United States would never enter the war and, like Wilhelm II before him, is reputed to have said, "Americans cannot swim. Americans cannot fly. Americans will never come." Americans proved him wrong and helped bring about the restoration of a balance of power in Europe upset by his march through Europe. The leadership of Franklin Delano Roosevelt in cautiously guiding American opinion toward confronting its responsibilities cannot be exaggerated. Roosevelt was unsure that the public would support American military initiatives. He hesitated, maneuvered, and bought time rather than act prematurely. He refused to engage the enemy before public support was at hand.

The time came, however, when others made the decision for FDR at Pearl Harbor. The Japanese attack on the United States was an act that was to "live in infamy." After the assault, the United States could no longer stand apart from the conflict. Earlier, it had shared its resources in coming to Britain's aid, and even that was done with a good deal of hesitation and soul-searching. There were several isolationist movements in the country, such as America First. Pacifist isolationist groups were prominent in religious circles. Indeed, the strongest opposition to U.S. participation in World War II came from church groups, liberal organizations, and business associations that insisted the country was being dragged into a conflict in which it had no interest. It was against that trend that Roosevelt and others had to fight.

Throughout the period, Niebuhr was in the forefront of those who supported American involvement in the struggle. He was persuaded that the United States had to play a role if Hitler was to be turned back. He was outspoken in challenging those who suggested that Hitler was no different from any other world leader. He opposed the view that morally no distinction was possible between Hitler's Germany and other nations. He argued that if Hitler were no different from the leaders of other nations, say, Britain or France, with trusteeships and colonies in Africa and Asia, then a moral distinction between leaders and nations was impossible at any time anywhere in the world. For Niebuhr, Hitler's acts were so cruel, repulsive, and barbaric—especially his assault on six million Jews and other minorities and his attacks on the smaller nations of Europe—that he had to be resisted. Niebuhr argued that the United States had to respond to this large-scale threat to all of Western Europe and perhaps the Western Hemisphere.

The ambiguity of Niebuhr's position, however, was that in the 1930s he had not been persuaded that Roosevelt or anybody else offered an answer to the question of security or the preparation of the United States for conflict. He voted twice against Roosevelt, and he thought of him as a trimmer and a compromiser—somebody who was unlikely to defend freedom. He voted twice for Norman Thomas—a socialist—and did so because he felt that socialism and leaders like Thomas offered a better chance of saving the American economy from destruction. Niebuhr feared the collapse of the American economy. He warned that capitalism was being destroyed in the United States and freedom endangered everywhere.

Niebuhr's perspective was confusing to some Americans because it seemed that Niebuhr was invoking the tenets of socialism and Marxism in order to save free enterprise. Those who lived through the Depression, however, may have forgotten, or some never knew, the severity of economic decline at the time. People who had been reasonably prosperous sold apples on the street. Others found their salaries and incomes cut by half or one quarter. A clear danger to the survival of the American economy led Niebuhr to conclude that draconian measures were needed to deal with the problem of human survival. The same problem was even more in evidence in Germany. The middle class was being forced down into the proletariat; it was identified as the *Lumpenproletariat*. Others referred to this group as the displaced middle class. The proletariat—who had once been the bourgeoisie or the middle class in Germany—turned to Hitler. With the precipitous decline of the economy, desperate people were proletarianized; they became indistinguishable from the traditional lower or working class. The *Lumpenproletariat* were attracted to Hitler because he promised to restore the economy and Germany to its rightful position of supremacy among the nations of Europe. That left other groups, such as the Jews and the Freemasons, as scapegoats charged with being responsible for Germany's problems and decline. Niebuhr took the challenge. He refused to sit idly by and let history repeat itself in the United States.

PUNDITS AND DIPLOMATS

Diplomats, generals, and journalists have also contributed to theories of international relations since antiquity. Thucydides, who in his *History of the Peloponnesian War* writes from the viewpoint of a general in that war, is one example, but foreign ministers such as Viscount Robert Stewart Castlereagh, Marquess of Londonderry, George Canning, and the French diplomats Jules and Paul Cambon also put their views to paper, and their principles are still relevant. What may, however, be different in our time is that beginning in the 1930s but reaching its fullest expression in the years after World War II, important journalists and diplomats produced books, articles, and papers that still rank with those of scholars and historians as contributions to international thought. George F. Kennan, Louis J. Halle, Walter Lippmann, James Reston, and E. H. Carr (in his journalistic writings) have contributed to international theory as well as to public understanding. The list could easily be expanded. It would include former secretaries of state Dean Acheson, Henry Kissinger, Dean Rusk, and George Shultz, as well as Paul H. Nitze, Dorothy Fosdick, Charles Bohlen, and George Ball, all of whom have written monographs or memoirs that merit study and consideration.

The influence of these men and women and their importance in the history of international thought stems in part from the range and scope of their writing and thinking. George Kennan, for example, is a historian of the Soviet Union, of Russia, and of American foreign policy. Louis Halle began his career as a nature writer. C. B. Marshall, who authored *The Limits of Foreign Policy*, Dorothy Fosdick, who wrote a small but valuable book on foreign policy, and Paul H. Nitze, whose writings in recent years have been voluminous, continue to be read, considered as dissertation subjects, and studied by those who seek to understand how practitioners view foreign policy.

In one sense, the role these individuals have played refutes the belief that there is an unbridgeable gulf between theorists and practitioners. It is sometimes said that theorists deal with eternal verities. Their focus is on the long view. They undertake to establish general principles of thought. As for practitioners, their purpose is to show those far removed from the realm of political or diplomatic experience what experience entails and how it differs from popular perception. Practitioners suggest that when theorists become practitioners they display weaknesses that result from lack of firsthand experience.

Sir Herbert Butterfield, the great British historian, is among those who have questioned whether theorists have much to contribute in practice. His favorite comment was, "Whenever I hear that some academic has been elevated to an important policymaking or policy implementation role, I get an unusually powerful headache." Critics see the theorist as more interested in doctrine than the do's and don'ts in foreign policy, in constructing concepts and principles more than in confronting issues on their merits, and in an abstract rather than a practical view of the universe of international relations. Practitioners often see themselves as working on problems within watertight compartments. They are the doers. They act on the basis of hunches rather than carefully formulated theories. They are contemptuous of those who deal in abstractions, because bringing forth and sustaining policy is not an intellectual but a practical exercise. Hard-pressed policy officials must shape policy as best they can, often with the hounds of time snapping at their heels. They do so with little conviction that what has been done before in foreign policy has much bearing on current problems.

In the views of some diplomatists, journalists, and pundits, a large question mark should follow a too-sharp division of American thinkers into theorists and practitioners. Dean Acheson, in an introduction to one of Louis Halle's early books, wrote that what a small group of theorists (including Halle) who had worked within the confines of the State Department were trying to do was to create a relevant body of theory for international relations. The implication was clear—that most theories concocted by persons who have lived their lives outside the realm of experience are impractical. Acheson went on to say that practitioners like Halle and Kennan were elaborating theories based on specific issues they had confronted. Not every issue carries forward the principles and lessons of the past. Some are unique events that happen only once. Problems appear without warning. Efforts to shape long-term theories have little relevance for the ongoing tasks of diplomatists.

In another connection, Dean Rusk once remarked that soon after he was appointed secretary of state by John F. Kennedy, the president and Rusk discussed the possibility of a generalized foreign policy for the United States. They concluded that no theory or grand design was possible that would help them to deal with tomorrow's problems. Nothing that offered a universal approach would help resolve a particular foreign-policy issue. In Rusk's words, when the president and his secretary of state face new problems, they usually must do so without the benefit of an overall concept of foreign policy based on history or past experience.

Despite reservations and a host of questions from respected intellectual leaders, diplomatists such as Kennan and Halle have persisted in laying down certain broad principles that may serve those who deal with policy. Among the principles they defend is that policymakers need an anchor to which they can attach their thinking, even though it may not provide readymade specific answers. In other words, they need a theoretical framework.

Among twentieth-century pundits with the greatest influence, Walter Lippmann occupies a special place at the top of almost every list. Under several headings, including "Today and Tomorrow," Lippmann wrote a thrice-weekly column that, for many, became a public-affairs bible. At Harvard, Lippmann as a student embraced socialism. He strongly supported Woodrow Wilson and was said to have been the architect of more than half of the Fourteen Points that constituted Wilson's defense of the League of Nations and of collective security. Then, suddenly, Lippmann turned against the Wilsonian approach. He said that Wilson's message was too much like the advice offered a young man by his father. The young man asks for guidance. The father replies, "Go forward." Going forward, however, is so vague and amorphous a directive that it provides little guidance. After his break with Wilson, Lippmann set off on an intellectual journey of his own. It was a journey that led him along the paths of differing ideas and philosophies. Like others who wrote in a period of economic decline in the United States, he was initially attracted by socialism. With Herbert Croly, he was a founder of the *New Republic*. He wrote regularly in the *New Republic*, and anyone interested in the development of his early thought can find it in the first numbers of that influential journal.

Lippmann explored a wide array of issues, among them public opinion. His writings were not calculated to offer testable propositions that could be measured through quantitative surveys. In Merriam's terms, they were not scientific. Instead, he saw public opinion as a vast and inchoate force in society at large. People had vague and unexamined ideas of what the nation ought to do that required definition and formulation. It remained for the leader to give them content. This was the role that a president, a prime minister, or leaders in other countries should perform.

At the same time, Lippmann talked about the boundaries and limitations of leadership. He said that the American people have placed an impossible burden on their presidents. A president must function as party leader, constitutional scholar, author of legislative programs, defender of the budget, and more. The sum of these responsibilities has made the presidential role virtually impossible to perform. What Lippmann was saying was what the Civil War general sought to express when he counseled his troops "to lower them sights." The public should lower its sights in its judgments of a president.

One of Lippmann's earlier books, written before World War II, bears most directly on contemporary foreign policy—*American Foreign Policy: Shield of the Republic.* In this little book Lippmann argues that for the first one hundred years or more of our history, we kept commitments overseas in balance with resources and means. Then beginning with Woodrow Wilson, we undertook commitments for which adequate resources were either lacking or not identified. In other words, we abandoned a hallowed tradition that for more than a century had marked our foreign-policy thinking, namely, that commitments and resources—ends and means—must be kept in balance. We ought never to set out to achieve a global or regional objective unless the military and economic resources to sustain such a policy are present or can be created. To this day, Lippmann's dictum regarding means and ends, commitments and resources, remains a revered precept of foreign policy surpassing in its wisdom what other theorists or practitioners have offered. That someone on the outside should have formulated a view of foreign policy which, with an economy of concepts and ideas, defined sharply what foreign policy was all about speaks volumes. An extraordinary outsider set forth a fundamental principle of foreign policy that is no less relevant today.

Lippmann's wider interests included the restoration of a public philosophy; his last book was devoted to the subject. In it he argued again that Americans in their early history had had a clear vision of the nation's purpose—and how to sustain it—embodied in a public philosophy. That vision entailed the search not only for a clearer view of the means of carrying out foreign policy but also a more profound view of what it was we stood for as a nation and a country. There had been early writings, beginning with the Founding Fathers and the authors of the *Federalist Papers,* on public-philosophy issues. Lippmann sought to renew that interest and make people think about what it was we sought as a country, not only in the realm of power but also with respect to purpose. Purpose required a deeper understanding of philosophical ends and a definition of ultimate goals. If we could develop a public philosophy, it would include a view of what Americans had to offer the world and the framework within which we made the offer.

A small group of diplomatists who were part of the policy-planning staff appointed by George F. Kennan and later Paul H. Nitze constitute a second body of thinkers from outside the academy who sought to formulate theories of international relations. Beginning in the 1950s, George Kennan, particularly in his book *American Diplomacy, 1900–1950,* tried to do precisely this. He set out to provide guidelines for the nation that could help it decide whether to undertake certain foreign policy initiatives. Americans, he said, are particularly vulnerable to a near-fatal disease. It has misled us, especially in foreign-policy undertakings. Kennan diagnosed the disease as moralism and legalism. We have a predilection for sweeping moralistic ideas in foreign policy, soaring global ideas that concern a world yet unborn but that we mistakenly think has been created by architects of peace plans, such as President Wilson and his predecessors.

So far as legalism is concerned, we have a penchant for legalistic thinking in our foreign policy. Our forefathers were the architects of a constitutional system. It is the most long lived of nearly all constitutional systems, matched only by early Polish and French constitutions. Constitutional thinking has encouraged us to believe that what has been carved out in the arena of domestic politics can equally well be established internationally. All we need is an international body such as an international court of justice—earlier it was the Permanent Court of International Justice—which, as it acquires more and more power and influence, can make decisions not on the basis of national political interest or national security concerns, but on the basis of what is legally right. One reason this view has had such sway in the United States is that a high proportion of our secretaries of state have been lawyers. Many key positions, including the undersecretary and the assistant secretary for international security affairs in the Defense Department, have been considered the province of lawyers who can carry out foreign policy tasks case by case and precedent by precedent in much the way they have proceeded within the domestic legal system. What the proponents of this view forget is that the precedent-oriented approach has never existed in international relations as it has domestically. In the international arena, *stare decisis* does not exist.

Nonetheless, hope dies slowly that a transformation of the political system to a system of law rather than a system of power is possible. Enthusiasm for international law has declined to the extent it has because a legalistic view is basically irrelevant in the great conflicts and contests for power in the international political sphere. If the Soviet-American conflict was to be settled at all, it likely would be settled by diplomacy, hard bargaining, compromise, and give-and-take rather than by an ofttimes nonexistent law for the problems at issue.

Kennan has continued his writing into his nineties, and his views still receive wide currency. As an author, he has earned wide acclaim through a Pulitzer Prize and a National Book Award. At the same time, he can be scathing in his views of others. Even those who have been somewhat close to him at one time or another have felt the bite of his criticism. He has never been especially gracious about the needs and thinking of his friends. Nevertheless, he remains a towering figure among historians and diplomatists and a writer who has few equals.

Louis Halle is another diplomat whose intellectual contribution must be placed firmly alongside that of academic writers. He was and is a marvelous writer. He first studied anthropology at Harvard University. He continued that interest in working with a railroad company in South America. He was a member of the policy-planning staff under George Kennan and Paul Nitze, respected and trusted by both. He wrote a series of books, all focusing in some way on broader concepts such as dream and reality in foreign policy and the Cold War as history. He has produced many other writings seeking to apply working concepts to international relations. Nonetheless, he has been critical of those he considers too abstract in their concepts. For whatever reason, he has received less acclaim than Kennan. He taught at the University of Virginia for a time after leaving the Department of State and then at the Geneva Institute of Graduate International Studies. He has always been respected for the rigor of his scholarship and his realistic approach to urgent problems.

Halle's thinking has put heavy emphasis on history—the history of American experience, American institutions, and American leadership. Halle likes to tackle large issues such as national-security planning and strategic thinking. He did this in particular after World War II, and his views represent some of the sharpest and most clearly delineated reflections on the subject. His *Cold War as History* remains a masterful exposition of the proposition that one cannot understand Soviet policy unless one understands czarist practice and pre-Bolshevik foreign policy. He acted as an independent scholar throughout most of his career, meeting his classes on schedule but remaining free from all the faculty maneuverings that occur within any institution of advanced learning—including the Graduate Institute of International Studies. He knew that politicking takes the place of scholarship. He participated in conferences in London and Paris and throughout Europe, where he presented his ideas on nuclear deterrence. This may represent his most important contribution. Halle's legacy resides in the collection of books he wrote on fundamental issues. It will always be valuable in this regard.

In a sense, the policy planning staff under Kennan and Nitze was unique. Four members (Kennan, Nitze, Halle, and C. B. Marshall) are authors who attracted international attention. They are remembered as much for their theories as they are for their policy making. Not only have two of them written as historians and critics, but each is also the author of a major foreign-policy doctrine that guided the nation through some intensely difficult years in the Cold War: Kennan was the principal author of containment, and Nitze, of NSC-68. Although containment was seen as more limitationist in practice than NSC-68, both the Truman Doctrine and NSC-68 were first presented as universalistic in character. In that connection, commentators over the years have discussed their thinking from the standpoint of underlying normative and political assumptions that were never made fully explicit.

KENNAN AND NITZE ON ETHICS AND FOREIGN POLICY

In 1993, two distinguished Americans published important books offering statements of their philosophies of foreign policy. One is George F. Kennan's *Around the Cragged Hill: A Personal and Po-*

litical Philosophy. The other is Paul H. Nitze's *Tension Between Opposites: Reflections on the Practice and Theory of Politics.* For half a century the two have provided an American version of the philosopher-statesman. Their thinking and writings reflect qualities that friends abroad find lacking among most U.S. policymakers. Kennan begins *Around the Cragged Hill* with the caveat that theory and abstractions are not his forte. He prefers the discussion of general beliefs through invoking specific examples. For him, it is a safer and less pretentious way of thinking. His motivation for undertaking to set forth his personal and political philosophy is to respond to those who call on him to be more explicit about his underlying political and ethical assumptions. He acknowledges that behind the propositions and issues he has advanced and discussed over the years may be generalizations that he should identify and make clear.

Nitze explains his motivation for writing *Tension Between Opposites* in more traditional academic terms. "Tension between opposites" was the theme of his graduate seminar at the School for Advanced International Studies at Johns Hopkins University. The focus was on the theory and practice of politics. Nitze asks whether it is possible to develop a framework of ideas that can illuminate past political problems and provide approximate guidelines for analogous problems in the future. His goal is to deduce from the experience and wisdom of earlier generations a theory of politics to serve future policymakers.

Science and Politics

A key issue that both Kennan and Nitze address is the role of science in providing answers to questions of politics. In discussing heredity and environment, Kennan expresses profound misgivings about what he describes as human manipulation through genetic engineering. For him, the two things that scientists should never attempt to bring under their control are weather and heredity. The fact that it is technically possible to recast human qualities through the scientific manipulation of human genes hardly justifies these experiments. In more general terms, Kennan replies to those who ask if, in questioning the march of science, he is not fighting science. Kennan calls upon his professional responsibility at the Princeton Institute for Advanced Studies to illustrate his respect for pure or basic science. In applied science, the epoch-making programs in the exploration of outer space and studies of the composition of matter are worthy of admiration. But if science's major contribution is to speed processes that are already too rapid—for example, in substituting robotic machines for human labor in societies overburdened by significant unemployment—Kennan opposes the effort. Trend should not be destiny in our appropriation of scientific advancements. In moving from scientific discovery to procurement and application, policymakers ought to weigh the consequences. In the study of politics and foreign policy, Kennan favors history and the humanities rather than behavioral or scientific inquiry.

At first reading, Nitze takes an unequivocal stand on science and declares that the study of politics can never be a science. A science presupposes certainty—at least within definable limits—made possible through repeatable tests and experiments. Political science since World War II has contributed little, however, because a science of politics is contrary to experience and common sense. In politics, Nitze doubts that repeatable experiments are possible, and he argues that analogies can only be suggestive. People live in different historical eras. The intensity of life and standards vary from one society to another. He reminds us that few had the opportunity to grow up in Pericles' Athens. As director of the State Department's policy planning staff, Nitze experienced for the first time the rewards of full participation in responsible decision making. It brought self-fulfillment. Yet, in looking back, he asks if he and his colleagues were right in holding steadfastly to Western values as superior to Marxist-Leninist-Stalinist claims. Were they right in judging that the United States was economically strong enough to carry out the role they assigned it? By what process of thought or what lessons of history or ethical criteria could such questions be answered? He concludes that judgments of this kind can be made only within some kind of moral and intellectual framework. On the place of historical analogies and their applicability in history, Nitze expresses hope mixed with uncertainty.

Man and Human Nature

Kennan, in much of his thinking, proceeds from the particular to the general. He turns to history, religion, and biology in search of evidence to overturn the notion that mankind is perfectible. He offers a portrait of government in which moral compromises in politics are unavoidable. They are burdens that officials must bear. What accounts for recurrence in history are certain congenital imperfections in human nature that affect everywhere the interior workings and external relations of the institutions of government and politics. Further, more permanent factors affect a country's ability to cope with its difficulties, including size. Kennan proposes a remedy that calls for dividing the nation into smaller units. Like other realists before him, he condemns the use of despairing words where courage is needed. There are few things in mankind's plight that cannot be alleviated but far fewer, if any, that can be cured. Religion and the humanities offer insights that lie beyond the reach of science. In a deeper sense, they provide perspectives on man and human nature that only the philosopher-scientist, as distinct from the specialist-scientist, is likely to understand.

Jakob Burckhardt called on philosophers and historians to return to the one central and irreducible reality on which all else is based: man. For Niebuhr and Burckhardt, the most vexing question is how we are to think of man and human nature. In none of his previous writings has Kennan addressed this question directly, nor has Nitze, who does not consider human nature as such, except in a brief reaction to Kennan's thought. In fact, one finds no reference to human nature in Nitze's index. It would be surprising if either Kennan or Nitze were to add much to what philosophers such as Burckhardt or Niebuhr have contributed. Nonetheless, Kennan feels obliged to address some of the central issues reflected in the title of his work and his portrayal of man as "the cracked vessel." He finds man's fatal flaw in his failure to shape behavior to the requirements of civilization. Man is the victim of the nearly irresolvable conflict between two powerful impulses in his nature. One is a quality he shares with the animals to preserve and propagate his own kind; the other is the imperative, reflected in the historical development of civilization, to redeem human life in part by introducing some measure of order, dignity, beauty, and respect—if not love—for fellow men. Man's soul is the battlefield in which the struggle between the two conflicting impulses is joined.

The compulsion to preserve and propagate the human race is

rooted in the "sexual urge," Kennan observes. He explains that the sexual urge needs no identification or description; it is the leading theme of most Western literature. No other aspect of the human condition inspires finer expressions of the human spirit. Yet however much it may accompany deep intimacy and profound devotion between individuals and provide satisfaction matched by few forms of human experience, it carries with it ambiguous effects, such as conflicting loyalties, jealousies, suspicions, and tragic unhappiness. Sex is a compulsion we share with the lowest and least attractive mammalian species. It invites furtive curiosity and commercial exploitation. Even profoundly moving and enriching intimacies can introduce "proprietary feelings" on the part of one or the other. (It is interesting to compare Hans J. Morgenthau's relating of love and power to Kennan's passing mention of "proprietary feelings," nor does Kennan have anything to say about AIDS or the criminal aspects of sex such as rape.) At best, it is a crude expression of nature's means for perpetuating the human race, intermingling joy, perplexity, confusion, and tragedy, and reflecting humanity's imperfection in the quest for a civilized life. In words reminiscent of a dispatch from the 1995 U.N. World Population Conference held in Cairo ("Whoever thought that talking about sex all week could be so boring"), Kennan describes the sexual act, absent its ennobling commitments, mysteries, and higher passions, as the most "tedious, monotonous, at times ridiculous, and least interesting of human proclivities."[1]

Self-love or self-regard is the other human dimension in the preservation of the race. In the words of Sigmund Freud, self-love is the source of man's "discomfort" in civilization. In advancing his own interests, he feels insecurity and uncertainty and seeks reassurance that he is in harmony with the legitimate aspirations of society. Thus, self-regard has a necessary and useful place in promoting self-respect and responsibility. It is threatened, however, from two sides—by underestimation of the person's qualities and by their overestimation. What Kennan calls *real* underestimation is induced by disappointments, failures, extreme sensitivity, and the toils of conscience, leading positively to a healthy moderation of aspirations and expectations but negatively to depression and despair. By contrast, feigned under-

1. George F. Kennan, *Around the Cragged Hill: A Personal and Political Philosophy* (New York, 1993), 19.

estimation takes the form of a false display of humility, insincere denial of self-value, and self-denigration. In 1879, in response to a younger brother who had signed his letter "your insignificant little brother," the Russian author Anton Chekhov wrote, "You are an honest fellow. Respect that in yourself. Don't confuse coming to terms with yourself with recognizing your insignificance."[2]

Overestimation of self is a more common attitude in which the reactions of others come into play. Man is a social animal, and try as he will, any wholly independent self-evaluation is impossible. Kennan recites the story, well known to his loyal readership, of being overwhelmed by the greater sophistication and easy self-confidence of fellow first-year students at Princeton. He fell ill and ultimately withdrew for a time. He tried to maintain his own standards but failed. He came to recognize that both self-evaluation and respect for the judgment of others is important. There is always a thirst for reassurance that others hold us in some measure of respect, but given man's doubts and uncertainty about himself, the thirst can never be fully satisfied. Particularly for someone in a position of prestige or authority, reassurance of this kind is a slippery slope. Outward respect or deference too easily becomes excessive flattery, and for someone as sensitive as Kennan—and perhaps for most people—deference is looked upon as a means of currying favor. He writes at length about flattery and the risks of its leading to conceit and posturing. Indulgence of the individual's self-regard leads to a lust for authority and a sense of undisguised superiority over others. It pervades personal and organizational life—even the family—and is sometimes confused with true leadership. Its most ruthless expression, however, is in formal associations and hierarchies such as professional, military, bureaucratic, and commercial organizations.

Self-regard that is good in moderation is not good when carried to extremes. Just as the sex drive often reflects human imperfection, so does self-regard. The individual is unable to accept reasonable limits. Perhaps because of disappointments in his own life and his failure to make himself understood in professional and personal relations, as in interpretations of his policies (Lippmann's devastating attack on containment policy is but one example), Kennan writes less

2. *Ibid.*, 22.

about the limitless search for increasing power with which Morgenthau and Niebuhr are concerned and more about the quest for power as a human flaw. Indeed, despite his high government service, he has little to say about the effective exercise of power as a necessity in government. Intellectually, he understands what the fathers of realism and Christian realism have addressed, as when he explains: "Because the authority of the one individual implies the subordination of another, because the expansion of one person's power implies the relative powerlessness of someone else . . . all manifestations of this thirst for authority and power involve rivalry." But for him the source of man's imperfections resides less in necessity and the basic traits of human nature than in discomfort in civilization. Humanity is ill at ease in society.

When Kennan returns to his original proposition—that man and, in particular, Western man, is a cracked vessel—he writes eloquently of some of the consequences of the tragic nature of man's imperfections: "Whipped around, frequently knocked off balance, by these conflicting pressures, he staggers through life as best he can, sometimes reaching extraordinary heights of individual achievement but never fully able to overcome, individually or collectively, the fissures between his own physical and spiritual natures." Yet it is not man's nature judged by objective standards outside history but the contradictions between his nature and the demands of civilization that are the root problem for Kennan. Thus his thesis about man as a cracked vessel suggests that man's "psychic makeup is the scene for the interplay of contradictions between the primitive nature of his innate impulses and the more refined demands of civilized life."[3] Such contradictions destroy the unity and integrity of man's undertakings and cause one part of his personality to be the enemy of another.

The West's greatest philosophers and theologians, including Niebuhr, see the human predicament in different terms. For Plato, the shadows on the cave point man, and especially philosophers, to the sun, which is the source and idea of objective truth. Niebuhr discovers objective reality in religious truths such as love. He writes of the impossibility of pure love in politics and society but of its

3. *Ibid.*, 26–27.

possibility as expressed in proximate justice within an imperfect society. In this sense, love is "the impossible possibility." Later, Kennan does speak of the soul or the spirit as a repository of virtue, but it is notable that in discussing human shortcomings and limitations, he finds that humanity in civilization—not objective principles—provides the evaluative standard. Amusingly, Kennan reinvents the little demon, in attendance on every civilized person, which leads him astray. Only saints, who have the power to drive out the disturbing little demon, and the truly great, whose virtues and strengths overshadow its disturbing influence, are immune from its sinister influence or are worthy of forgiveness.

Nitze addresses the question of human nature in his own way. He finds Kennan's analysis too tragic a view of mankind. Without mentioning human nature, he recommends that we look at what he calls "the problem" through the lens of the complementarity of opposites or the tension between truth, beauty, and life. It is the tensions between man's humanity and the constraints of the culture of which he is a part that "produce the rich life that makes it worth living."[4] Throughout his career, Nitze has tended to identify evil in the world not with human imperfection and shortcomings but with totalitarian regimes and powerful ideological forces that threaten the world. According to his enemies, the one exception for which he received criticism involved his own highly profitable investments in the 1930s in Germany, pursued despite the impending rise of Hitler. He has a credible answer to this criticism and what is called a misreading of the history of his investments.

Nitze recounts a story that is revealing. It builds upon a satire, *This Simian World*, by Clarence Day. Supreme Court Justice Oliver Wendell Holmes had advised Dean Acheson, who considered Holmes his intellectual hero, that the satire contained more insight into human nature than many volumes of philosophy. The simians triumphed over other animals; they were better qualified to rule because of desire and adaptability. Curiosity was for them a "master passion," but they also came to know who they were and were not caught up in unrealistic expectations or artificial ideas. Humans run

---

4. Paul H. Nitze, *Tension Between Opposites: Reflections on the Practice and Theory of Politics* (New York, 1994), 132.

the risk of adopting standards that are too distant and exalted. We should discover what to do being who we are.

Nitze read *This Simian World* and was impressed. It brought back memories from college days of a gypsy palmist and a girl named Anna Scott in whom he had a romantic interest. She and her friends were intrigued by palmistry. He joined her in visiting a palm reader who stared at Nitze's hand for five minutes without speaking. Finally, she said, "I can say nothing about this man. He has a purely practical hand." Nitze maintains that his skepticism about mystics, prophets, and revealed truth springs from his practical nature. He goes on to say that his skepticism carries with it confidence in the human mind and in the ability to reason, to foresee and estimate the consequence of actions, and to judge between the better and the worse, rather than the good and the bad—a distinction that is too absolute for simian beings. Yet at the same time, Nitze expresses disappointment at Acheson's skepticism toward attempts to generalize about the structure of political situations and the interrelation of causal factors. Acheson was not, however, devoid of beliefs, as suggested by his embracing the Greek definition of happiness—"the exercise of vital powers along lines of excellence, in a life offering them scope."[5] The tension between the opposites of skepticism and belief made Acheson a successful and joyous man.

It is leaders and statesmen he has known that capture Nitze's attention far more than abstractions about human nature, and perhaps they offer the best clue to his thinking. He devotes some 110 pages of *Tension Between Opposites* to profiles and character studies of seven outstanding Americans who exercised their powers along lines of excellence in "lives offering them scope." For Nitze, two of them provide examples of the practice of politics (Truman and Forrestal). One exemplifies virtue and competence (Clayton). Kennan illustrates the nexus between theory and practice. Acheson displays the virtues and limitations of elegance. George C. Marshall embodies the practice of democracy, and George Shultz personifies loyalty. Nitze is at his best in sketches of these seven remarkable men whom he knew and served with during a half century of momentous decision making.

5. *Ibid.,* 153–54.

Remembering Truman from the days in which he was identified with the Pendergast political machine in Kansas City, Nitze was skeptical about his ability to lead. Truman's caution in handling General MacArthur made Nitze uneasy. Yet when the British announced they could no longer support Greece and Turkey, Truman acted decisively with the Truman Doctrine, the Marshall Plan, and NATO. Truman's strengths derived in part from his sense of history. His high-school teacher taught him Greek and Roman history, and he developed respect for the responsibilities of high office. When asked if he were not in awe of the intellectual powers of men like Marshall and Acheson, he answered, "As Harry Truman I'm nothing; as President of the United States I'm everything." Many public officials shrink from the responsible use of power. Truman realized self-fulfillment in its deployment. For Nitze, it is a given that the leader must both think and act. He should be more than a paradigm of the ideals of his time. Through him, ideals can be renewed and extended. Truman communicated the sense of the leader's responsibility to his oath of office, and he transmitted an American political philosophy that enabled him to meet a host of challenges in a troubled postwar world.

If responsibility to office is the message of Harry Truman, the will to succeed is the legacy of James Forrestal, who was secretary of the navy and later secretary of defense under Truman. He was a man fully engaged in the practice rather than the theory of politics. Forrestal credits the blacksmith in a neighboring town with having taught him that will was everything. Will, courage, and persistence are essential virtues in politics. Forrestal's rise to power was driven by passion, but he learned to his sorrow that single-mindedness depends on the political strategic situation. Forrestal's determination to succeed outweighed loyalties to family, church, and party. It overcame his natural instinct to help friends and associates. Yet when his friends deserted him and critics vilified him, his mind and will failed him. In the absence of success, he lost his passion and his life.

Will Clayton was a man of true virtue and practical wisdom. He combined the virtues of husband, father, citizen, and public servant: competent, hardworking, believing in his country and its people, and knowing the world and its needs. He was a prosperous cotton merchant whom Roosevelt first hesitated to appoint because he had contributed twenty-five thousand dollars to the Republican party. Once appointed, he tackled wartime shortages of both raw materials and trained manpower. He became undersecretary of state for economic affairs and made the economic recovery of Europe his highest immediate priority, but the worldwide reduction of trade barriers was his long-run goal. In memoranda and cables from Europe, he outlined the main facets of what was to become the Marshall Plan, including the amounts of money required year by year, its division among principal recipients, and the local-currency counterpart of U.S. aid. All this he did while restricting his contacts with the press until Joseph Alsop wrote a column based on conversations with Paul Nitze entitled "The Clayton Cables." He sought no honors for himself but earned the nation's highest honors.

Late in July, 1943, Nitze met George F. Kennan for the first time on a crowded train en route from New York to Washington. That meeting was the beginning of a long friendship. Despite their differences, Nitze pays tribute to Kennan by observing that most of his ideas on the formulation of policy were either stimulated by or borrowed from Kennan or produced in reaction to Kennan's proposals that he considered impractical. Kennan's "Long Telegram," which described the Soviet government and foreign-policy objectives, and its translation into policy by the State, War, Navy Coordinating Committee (SWNCC) report under Kennan's guidance impressed Nitze as a penetrating review of the Leninist-Stalinist doctrine. The first signs of significant differences between Kennan and Nitze came with the possibility of the early removal of Soviet and Western forces from Germany, including Berlin. They differed on U.S. responses to the explosion of the first Soviet atomic bomb. On NSC-68, both Kennan and Bohlen argued that the doctrine overestimated the probability of Moscow-inspired military aggression and Soviet/Chinese military capabilities. With the invasion of South Korea, Nitze considered his doctrine confirmed. Nitze's highest tribute to Kennan was that he helped show the world that Americans recognized not only our material prosperity and scientific progress but also our ability to understand the other side of world issues and characteristic weaknesses such as "greed, corruption, and intellectual illiteracy." He had called for the renewal of American virtue and self-sacrifice by his words and his life.[6]

6. *Ibid.*, 132.

Nitze portrays Dean Acheson as a close friend but only after Nitze left government and retired as director of the policy planning staff. As a colleague, Nitze looked up to and admired Acheson. Earlier, they had sometimes disapproved of each other. In profiling Acheson, Nitze writes of the virtues and limitations of elegance. When Nitze came to Washington from Wall Street, his first assignment was with the Foreign Economic Administration, which Acheson charged had encroached on the State Department's authority in the economic field, an invasion he attributed principally to Nitze. Acheson's accomplishments from 1949 to 1953 were, however, gloriously productive. To serve with him was sheer joy. He was at his best working with staff. He encouraged them, protected them when attacked politically, kept them informed even about his talks with the president, and made them feel part of his and the president's team. He knew how to head into problems, not shy away from them. He did not wilt under pressure. He did not concentrate on one problem to the exclusion of an overall strategic view. Acheson was skeptical of any attempt to generalize and develop some kind of intellectual framework for understanding politics, but he balanced his skepticism with a passionate belief in the practice of excellence. He believed command and leadership gave scope for excellence. One wonders why in his book Nitze used the title "The Virtues and Limitations of Elegance" in reference to Acheson.

Everyone who had the opportunity to work with or for General George C. Marshall held him in the highest regard. He believed in taking action, even with imperfect knowledge. His favorite expression was, "Don't fight the problem." A leader and a people could learn only from acting, but the corollary was a willingness to adjust one's course promptly when new and better information became available. He advocated assigning full responsibility to a designated official and giving that person the authority to take action without expecting detailed guidance. Nitze worked with Marshall in 1940 and 1941 in preparing the country's defense program. It was a lesson in how the American democratic process can work at its best. The draft had both to be and to appear to be fair, and to be understandable and administered at the grassroots level by local people whom the draftees knew and trusted. Marshall went before Congress to defend the defense plan. He inspired problem solvers from Wall Street who had little understanding of the political constraints of the democratic system in which he had labored and lived most of his life. The Selective Service Act passed Congress by one vote and was signed into law on September 16, 1940. Marshall played the decisive role in its passage.

George Shultz exemplified the quality of loyalty. He was the principal force in negotiations with the Soviet Union during the Reagan administration. He was a business executive who had been president of Bechtel and professor of economics at MIT, Chicago, and Stanford. He had also been secretary of labor, director of the Office of Management and Budget, and secretary of the treasury in the Nixon administration. Eighteen months into President Reagan's first term, he replaced Alexander Haig as secretary of state. He supported negotiators such as Nitze when Reagan's national security adviser, William Clark, sought to restrict Nitze's contacts with anyone but the president and himself. After his famous "walk in the woods," Nitze found the secretary of state to be his chief ally, if not a rescuer of Nitze's formula. Shultz knew how to delegate responsibility to staff and subordinates and expected them to take initiatives. He drew on their knowledge for important meetings with Gorbachev, Gromyko, and Shevardnadze.

In negotiating with Gorbachev, Shultz used the issue of human rights to the advantage of the United States. He was comfortable with himself and knew his strengths and limitations. He knew how to reduce tensions in East-West negotiations with such answers as, "on matters of foreign policy of course I am always right," at the very moment Gorbachev attacked him for thinking he was always right. Gorbachev broke into laughter. Because of his confidence, Shultz sometimes retained staff who held sharply divergent views, and Nitze mildly criticizes him for that. He emphasized team play and cut back on bureaucratic infighting. He gave and received loyalty to his staff, and his integrity won their trust.

If there is a common element or unifying theme in the pantheon of leaders Nitze evaluates, it is virtue. Whereas Kennan invokes history and humanities in his portrayal of human nature, Nitze calls upon the Greek view of self-fulfillment through participation in the American polity. Although he would not claim expertise in Greek political thought, Nitze makes significant references to Plato and

Heraclitus. He takes pride in the pursuit of practical wisdom reminiscent of the Greek concept of prudence. Two of the heroes who impress him most are Truman and Forrestal, and both are remembered for the practice of politics. Truman's respect for the presidency and his sense of responsibility and ability to act decisively set him apart. With Forrestal, the will to act effectively and his courage and persistence are master virtues, even though both his will and his courage were shattered in the tragic ending of his life. Will Clayton was the personification of the virtue of believing in his country and quietly laying the foundations for an American policy to restore Europe and enhance world trade. Nitze's profile of Kennan describes the historian-diplomat's contributions to the theory of international relations and the formulation of postwar foreign policy but notes his shortcomings in the realm of practice. Dean Acheson shared with Truman the ability to act and to work effectively with others. He knew how to head into a problem, and he believed in the pursuit of excellence, especially in the exercise of command and leadership. With all his many qualities, General Marshall's greatest strength, in Nitze's eyes, was his understanding of democracy and its political constraints. He believed in acting even with imperfect information, learning and adapting as he acted. George Shultz's greatest strength was loyalty to his staff and negotiators. He knew himself and his strengths and limitations, and like Marshall, he made mistakes and went on. He was not afraid to delegate and urge staff initiatives by those who were competent.

Responsibility, decisiveness, the will to act, virtue, practical wisdom, theoretical insights, excellence, democracy, and loyalty are virtues the exceptional leader can attain within the political arena. Whereas Kennan's concern is with certain limitations of human nature, Nitze finds human potential in men who act. In the interaction between these two remarkable Americans, we can move a little closer to an understanding of human nature and politics and foreign policy.

Ethics and Foreign Policy

In 1950, Ambassador Kennan in his book *American Diplomacy* warned that legalism and moralism were powerful tendencies in American foreign policy that led those responsible for the conduct of foreign policy astray. He sought to limit the impulse of Americans toward national self-righteousness. In his discussion of government, he returns to this theme, observing that "the institution of government bears, in essence, no moral quality." Although government saves mankind from self-destruction, it is "morally neutral," and the same can be said of most of the functions of government, such as the maintenance of law and order, diplomacy and national defense, and the regulation of competing and conflicting economic interests. As with government, they are necessities but, for Kennan, rather sad necessities, stemming from the inability of men and women to govern themselves in a manner compatible with the interests of the community as a whole.

That government must direct its attention to such uninspiring needs ought not lead to its disparagement. The process of governance is worthy of respect, but Kennan questions whether it should be idealized. It is not the realm in which man's noblest impulses are realized. Instead, the tasks of government more often involve constraining the ignoble traits of mankind that appear in life and in society and must be kept from going too far. Politicians and those skilled in public relations may present their efforts as wholly directed toward high and exalted ends. In fact, at their best they fall short of the moralistic claims that are made for them by power-hungry individuals.

Recalling political philosophers such as Machiavelli, Aristotle, and Augustine, Kennan revives the distinction between necessity and choice. Of World War I he had written, "You could not say that anyone had deliberately started the war or schemed it." Man acts from either necessity or choice, and only with choice can an act be moral. All governments, whether democratic or nondemocratic, function in an atmosphere of "inflamed ambitions, rivalries, sensitivities, anxieties, suspicions, embarrassments and resentments." Government, for unavoidable reasons, is a necessary but unpleasant business. For all these reasons, it should be viewed by outsiders with "a sigh for its unquestionable necessity" and by the participant with "a prayer for forgiveness for the many moral ambiguities it requires him to accept and for the distortions of personality it inflicts upon him."[7] As for the pursuit of excellence in a life offering unparalleled scope,

7. George F. Kennan, *American Diplomacy, 1950–1990* (Chicago, 1951), 58; Kennan, *Around the Cragged Hill,* 209–10, 251–59, 53–58.

Kennan sees mainly the darker side of government, including rivalries, anxieties, and the distortion of personality, perhaps reflecting some of his own experiences and disappointments for which he (at least in part) has sometimes been held responsible.

As with anyone who seeks to understand the source and reality of moral choice, Kennan struggles to provide an explanation. He speculates that at some crucial point in the development of the human race, mankind was subject to a change that other forms of life did not experience. Man developed a capacity for self-awareness and an understanding of the moral qualities of his own behavior. He acquired an ability to distinguish, however imperfectly, between right and wrong. The change must have been very gradual and part of an evolutionary process. It set man apart from the beasts. None of man's limitations, then or now, are an expression of moral delinquency passed on by his ancestors. Even symbolically, Kennan rejects the idea of original sin, and he makes the rejection repeatedly, leading him to the point where he seems overly concerned to distinguish his outlook from that of more traditional religious viewpoints.

When Kennan turns to morality and foreign policy, he once again begins by saying that despite repeated efforts, he has been misunderstood. After 1950, when in *American Diplomacy* he had "casually mentioned" moralistic preaching and excessive legalism, he was interpreted as advocating cynical and amoral policies for the United States. In a *Foreign Affairs* article (Winter, 1985–86), he sought to clarify his views, but very few readers were satisfied with his answers. In that article he made a distinction between agent and principal and argued that government as agent, guided by moral convictions, was not the same as that of the individual as principal in the decisions he had to make. Surprisingly, in illustrating his views on morality and foreign policy, Kennan goes no further than reiterating his well-known opposition to secret intelligence operations while justifying once again his view that the process of negotiations must be private, even though the results must be made public.

In words that reflect a kind of final resignation he declares, "Beyond these observations, I am disinclined to resume the rather fruitless discussion of the relationship between morality and foreign policy." He explains he had had no luck in past efforts. He does, however, offer a few civilizing principles for the nation to follow in its policies. They include patience and an accommodating spirit in relations with small countries and in small matters; reasonableness and consistency with larger states; dignity and moderation of expression in official exchanges with other governments; and putting one's own house in order as a model of decency, humanity, and success for others to emulate if they wish. Every regime, he reminds us, speaks with two voices: one for all the people and the other for its own interests. If one were to confront politicians of either party and ask why they seem to give far more attention to electoral concerns, they would answer they could not speak in terms of the national interest without having first gained or renewed their mandate for political office and power.[8] They explain that a statesman is often a dead politician. Kennan's answer is that for most politicians, domestic political concerns too often crowd out national goals and purposes and the interests of the nation as a whole.

Nitze, at first glance, appears more determined than Kennan to explore ethics and foreign policy in some depth. Especially in the first part of *Tensions Between Opposites*, he stakes out a much broader field of action than in his earlier writings. At the outset, he makes clear his impatience with those who discuss the nature of man, an approach he questions and rejects in a single sentence. Nor do those who seek to interpret the behavior or psychology of man receive any more favorable recognition. Those who stress individual self-interest or group survival tend to exacerbate rather than resolve political conflict. These are complex issues in political life that must be judged from a point of view that transcends self-serving motives. We are told that the foundation of political theory and political practice must be "objective, universal, and in part altruistic." Having categorically denied the possibility of a science of politics, Nitze shifts his ground somewhat when he proposes that twentieth-century "developments in modern science and their implications for philosophy" offer hope in the search for an ethical perspective. Today's scientists understand the limits of science and recognize that subjects not covered by their scientific concepts must be "should" propositions. An ethical view not in conflict with science is now possible.

Nitze also takes heart from developments in philosophy and, in

8. *Ibid.*, 208–209, 60–61, 208–10.

particular, ontology, epistemology, and logic that are changing ancient definitions of truth. Few thinkers any longer accept the ideas of the logical positivists, including the notion that truth can be discovered through subjecting hypotheses to repeatable scientific experiments. As confidence in the thoroughgoing study of the material universe has diminished, students of the concepts and roles of such topics as purpose, relation, mediation, probability, and chance have put forward new ideas. They postulate that the "reality" of general ideas like justice or duty is no different than that of concepts in nuclear physics. Such modes of thought, to which Nitze makes few, if any, references in his profiles of living Americans discussed above, cast a long shadow of doubt on older ways of thinking about man and nature. In words reminiscent of behavioral thinkers such as Morton Kaplan almost forty years ago, Nitze predicts that it is possible to take a major step forward in ethical thinking. He is euphoric about the possibility of "an ethical framework within which [man] can reach more objective judgments concerning choices among values and value systems."[9]

Where can we look for the source of human activity? Nitze discovers the source in man's sense of living and being and the gradual discovery of a specific potential inherent in being. (Aristotle called man's potential his *telos,* but curiously, Nitze passes over the Aristotelian view without mentioning this crucial concept in the history of thought. With a few exceptions, Nitze identifies political theorists he respects by name but is strangely silent about exploring their views in depth.) Man's sense of being and self-awareness contribute to a natural sense of purpose.

For Nitze, history repeats itself only in a general sense, and the precedents it offers for decisions and actions are not unambiguous. Therefore, we must seek an integration of general concepts of purpose and direction with concrete issues and possibilities in the present. In the past fifty years, changes in thinking about the theory and practice of politics have become changes in kind. Nitze believes that the development of a more deeply and objectively based theory is possible. He selects four thinkers who from his viewpoint have contributed to a breakthrough in ethical thought. The first is Quentin

9. Nitze, *Tension Between Opposites,* 43.

Hogg, later Lord Hailsham. In *The Door Wherein I Went* Hailsham makes a case for what he calls natural morality, expressed in general guidelines such as "tell the truth," "love your country," "do not murder, steal, or lie." Nitze admits there are exceptions and limitations to the guidelines but seems impressed by their positive nature. They express a concern with how to act rather than how not to act.

Natural morality for Hailsham has another virtue. It provides a corrective to nineteenth-century ideas of law. Writers then adopted a wholly formal definition of law as being the command of the ruler. Those who employ such concepts of jurisprudence seem unaware of Hitler's definition of law: "Das ist recht was dem Führer gefällt" (What the führer says, is law). Hailsham insists that something more than a ruler's dictate is required to make law. A natural morality must underlie political activity. It provides guidance and justice at every level. Nitze is attracted to natural morality as a foundation for credible value judgments because one can come to it unassisted by divine revelation or the authoritative pronouncements of some group. He sees it related to what he has called "objectively based theory." But he leaves unanswered how flawed human beings, unschooled and unabetted, can produce natural morality.

Isaiah Berlin served in the British Embassy in Washington during World War I, and Nitze, Charles Bohlen, and the Alsops struck up an acquaintance with him. Berlin's early work was on nineteenth-century Russian intellectual ideas and on Wittgenstein and the neopositivists. Later, he turned his attention to values in collision. Liberty and equality are two of the primary goals of humanity, but they must be seen in relationship with each other. Total liberty for wolves is death to the lambs. Politics involves the balancing of values. All we can do is soften the collision of values. Berlin saw no ultimate solution to the problem. He saw civility and decency as values appropriate to all political action. Nitze asks, "Appropriate to Lenin, Hitler, and Saddam Hussein?" Nitze believes only toughmindedness, if not force, is appropriate in relations with such leaders. He is less impressed with the collision than the imperative of values.

Berlin introduced Nitze to the writings of Joseph de Maistre and to *The Origins of Fascism.* De Maistre challenged Enlightenment thinkers for their optimism and rationalism. They suffer from illusions. Men, or particular men, are savage and brutal. Man seeks to maximize his pleasures and minimize his pains. He is a self-destructive creature who acts only in accordance with individual interest. Man's first need is for his growing reason to be put under the yoke of the church and state. Man should lose himself in the raison d'état so that his individual reason may become communal reason. Man's nature presupposes violence, dark forces, and the glorification of chains as alone being capable of curbing self-destructive instincts. De Maistre appeals to blind faith rather than reason. He embraces the doctrine of blood and self-immolation, believes in the national soul, and warns against the subversive influence of uncontrolled intellectuals. Nitze believes de Maistre's ideas are at the heart of modern totalitarianism. He is the intellectual forebear of antirationalism and brutal ideology. Although he seeks a better understanding of ideology and its roots, de Maistre awaits the appearance of evil and proposes unacceptable measures to head it off. Nitze questions whether Berlin's attention to de Maistre is justified or whether de Maistre has any relevance for ethics and foreign policy. In principle at least, de Maistre is Nitze's least favorite theorist.

Milton Heifetz, on the other hand, appears to be Nitze's philosopher of choice with respect to ethics and foreign policy. Heifetz bases his theory on mankind's universal desire to avoid harm. From this concept he derives four principles that, taken together, make up a negative formulation of the Golden Rule: Do not do unto others that which you would not wish them to do unto you—hardly original with Heifetz. Heifetz and Nitze consider this a less-demanding rule than the Judeo-Christian precept that one should love one's neighbor as oneself. It has found much wider support. The concept can be found in all religions, including Judaism, Islam, historical Christianity, Buddhism, Confucianism, and Hinduism. Heifetz goes on to add four universal precepts for ethical behavior:

1. Do no harm.
2. Enjoy freedom—as long as others are not hurt by that freedom.
3. Practice beneficence—defined as action taken for the good of another person, perhaps from a variety of motives. It is distinguished from benevolence, which involves the motivation to do good; benevolence is more in tune with the positive Golden Rule.

4. Act for the common good. It is our duty.

Heifetz affirms that national sovereignty is inviolate until formal action to transgress it is authorized through what he calls due process, regardless of the internal structure of another nation, the immorality of its leadership, and the degree of oppression used to establish its governing body. Without some form of due process, all physical intervention must be taboo. Sanctions and economic pressure are not prohibited, however, although Heifetz makes no attempt to identify any existing source of due process for such acts. He suggests that joint action and agreement between the United Nations and the World Court would fulfill the concept of objective due process. Yet given their history, he hardly explains how they might act together. He acknowledges that serious problems arise in attempts to develop objective and testable standards under which cruel and inhuman actions by nations may be compared. Heifetz recommends that the State Department and the Congress begin to inculcate his four moral principles throughout government.

Nitze asserts that three of the four thinkers he discusses—Hailsham, Berlin, and Heifetz—are in agreement that most men are not entirely self-seeking. (Curiously, Nitze sometimes speaks of totalitarian regimes in language reminiscent of de Maistre.) Men strive to reach out beyond themselves to help others "within limits." Nitze asks readers to return to his framework for dealing with these issues. The heroes of Nitze's framework are the members of what he calls the "we" group, of which he considers himself a member. They are the ones who can act along the lines Heifetz has outlined against members of the "they" group. In the meeting of the "we" and "they" groups, the former must take account of the facts of the situation in which the action takes place. These facts include geography, demography, the state of scientific and technological knowledge, and conditions of economic, military, and political development at home and abroad. The situation provides the common ambience in which interchange between the "we" and "they" group occurs. The observer evaluating their interrelation will require a comprehensive theory of politics of the type Nitze provides. His theory, Nitze maintains, offers a better way of studying ethics and foreign policy than the writings of the great thinkers whose work he has earlier dismissed.

One reason Nitze is attracted to Heifetz' quite general propositions is because Heifetz denies that foreign affairs must ever be amoral to be successful. Morality can be productive of world harmony and peace. Heifetz condemns classical realists, especially Thucydides, Machiavelli, and Hobbes, but he reserves his strongest criticism for Reinhold Niebuhr. He maintains that Niebuhr's concept of morality led to the perpetuation of an amoral approach to foreign affairs, and Morgenthau and Kennan followed in this vein. Heifetz' main point is that Niebuhr based his concept of ethics on a flawed interpretation of religious morality in which unselfishness is the criterion of highest morality. Heifetz has little interest in the search for higher standards. He argues instead that secular morality does not require what he calls unlimited unselfishness, but only the obligation to do good provided it does not demand too great a sacrifice. Heifetz' four principles, then, are nonmaleficence, freedom, beneficence, and the common good, which are applicable to individuals and groups within a secular pluralistic nation but also to foreign affairs.

In foreign affairs, to which he turns in conclusion, Heifetz argues in ways hardly consistent with his moralistic views cited above that we must accept three concepts as givens:

1. Governments are inclined to pursue self-centered interests contrary to the interests of other nations.
2. The community of nations exists not only for the good of all nations but is also considered by individual nations to exist primarily for the good of the individual nation.
3. No nation's right to act vis-à-vis another is unlimited and unqualified.

What are we to make of the efforts of these two immensely talented policy advisers? What do they give us that previous theorists leave out? How seriously are we to take their "adventure into morality and foreign policy"? How accurate is their portrayal of past thinkers and of current philosophers and diplomats whom they seem to embrace? Why does one say he will not try again to make people understand his views and the other espouse a rather fragmentary and unconventional approach to the subject presented by a somewhat obscure Israeli philosopher? These are the issues that should be discussed in thinking about Kennan and Nitze on ethics and foreign policy.

CONCLUSION

In their efforts to contribute to thinking on ethics and foreign policy, Kennan and Nitze come close at points to bridging the gulf between theorists and practitioners. Each is more at home in both areas than the vast majority of practitioners tend to be. Looking back, they express crucial differences with Dean Acheson, who believed that the Department of State seldom if ever had received help from "academically or analytically minded men." On the contrary, both Kennan and Nitze have turned to academic consultants. Nitze in particular, however, has worried about the tendency of theorists toward abstraction and generalization and the use of historical analogies. Practitioners are no less guilty, and their use of the Munich analogy is among the most egregious examples of false analogies.

Few would question that theorists and practitioners often fail to explain the basis for their actions. The British statesman Lord Franks "found that the most prevalent single cause of misunderstanding and suspicions . . . [is] failure to communicate the assumptions of a proposal." Practitioners are particularly at fault in this respect. President Nixon liked to say that policymakers had to be empiricists and pragmatists acting case by case. John Foster Dulles often said he would welcome assistance from academics who had knowledge and experience comparable to his but asked, "Where are there such people?" Theorists can be excused for returning the compliment.

The simple truth is that we can point at most to a few policymakers who were both theorists and practitioners. The authors of the *Federalist Papers* fall into this category, for some were as learned in the great texts as they were skilled in the practice of governance. Lincoln, though self-taught, must be seen in the company of the founders. From 1936 to 1939, Churchill wrote a series of fortnightly letters on foreign policy. In one, he asserted that "those who are possessed of a definite body of doctrine and of deeply rooted convictions upon it will be in a much better position to deal with the shifts and surprises of daily affairs."

Kennan and Nitze hardly approach the level of these statesmen-philosophers. Kennan is too self-conscious of the need to distinguish his own mode of thinking to share in any depth ideas he has drawn from historians and philosophers. At most, he recognizes a concept or two he has found useful, for example, Niebuhr's "self-regard." As for Nitze, he proceeds on the basis of a random selection of the best minds he has encountered, but there is not much evidence of any identifiable influence on his own thinking in practice, nor is there the likelihood that certain minor figures to whom he has recourse will have any lasting importance in the history of thought. Indeed, the major political thinkers whom Nitze criticizes are thinkers such as Isaiah Berlin and de Maistre, who already have earned a place in the history of thought.

Thus Kennan and Nitze have, at best, had limited success in narrowing the cleavage between theory and practice. In consequence, they leave the problem of ethics and foreign policy more or less where they found it. They afford us an opportunity to explore in greater detail their analysis of ethical thinking, but it would be an exaggeration to say they have transformed the field. When two experienced and serious practitioners encounter obstacles they cannot surmount, the limitations of lesser writers are that much more understandable. Compared with Niebuhr, for example, Kennan and Nitze are as children setting forth on a new journey but lacking the intellectual and philosophical equipment to reach their goal. Nonetheless, we learn from them because of their lasting contributions in other areas and their courage in grappling with the great issues, however fateful the effort.

III

ISSUES

ATTITUDES: OPTIMISM, PRACTICE, AND PEACE

International relations involves hard choices, and those who must live with its realities ought not to assume it will be otherwise. In three important respects, however, crucial international-relations choices can be made either more intractable or more attainable than popularly understood. We can approach foreign policy and the modalities of choice against the background of three attitudes or ways of thinking about choice. They are optimism and/or realism, theory and/or practice, and force and/or peace. These three options and the underlying assumptions guiding those who embrace each approach make for a lively debate that is inevitably controversial and hard fought. It seems unlikely, given the controversies over the attitudes and philosophies of choice, that the issues they raise will disappear anytime in the foreseeable future.

The first approach to choice involves a powerful American attitude and idea—optimism. We are told that optimism and change are the two factors that hold most appeal in presidential elections. If a leader brings optimism onto the political scene, followers are likely to go further in accepting the attendant sacrifices and consequences. Optimism is the belief that however difficult a present choice may be, some future choice will be easier or better or more promising. Optimists say that realists deal only with the gloomy side of foreign-policy choices. Optimism points the way to the future, and reformist movements inspire people to act on the basis of hope. Indeed, those who must choose tend toward either optimism or realism. The idea that optimism alone can quickly transform the intractable problems of international relations is in dispute. It has been questioned down through the ages.

Examples abound of conflicts that optimists say ought not to have occurred. Athens and Sparta ought never to have fought the Peloponnesian War. One was a trading nation and the other militaristic and warlike. They should have been able to discover reinforcing common interests in which one would have drawn on the resources and strength of the other. A rough equilibrium of power was possible among the Greek city-states much as it should have been possible in the heart of Europe prior to World War I. Both sides, even in the face of the assassination of the Archduke Ferdinand in Sarajevo, should have resisted the temptation to rush into conflict.

Optimism sees new institutions creating a new world order. Optimism is based on the expectation that however difficult present relationships may be, they are bound to be better tomorrow. Optimism is mother's milk for hard-pressed men and women who go to work every day. If they can look toward a better day and a more hopeful future, however small their attention to international relations, they can be positive and optimistic about the future.

Realism questions whether optimism alone provides an effective escape from the challenge of dealing with harsh reality. Furthermore, what is optimism? What can one say about its elements and components? Optimism is oftentimes based on the foolish hopes of rank amateurs as they turn their attention to the distant arena of international politics. Optimism can be seen as an ideology in substitution for a viable foreign policy. We sometimes speak of the ideology of optimism as "blind optimism." One closes one's eyes to what may lie ahead and dismisses all thought about what needs to be done in the present. This kind of blind optimism in the history of international relations has plagued the lives of almost all nations, including the United States. It was blindly optimistic for the United States in the period between two world wars to assume that it could play a role in world peace by retreating from world politics. It is blindly optimistic for present-day Americans to assume we need have nothing to do with the former Soviet Union, with China, or with other major areas in the world. That scarcely justifies an extremist policy by the United States of sending unlimited resources into areas where the prospects of constructive use are unlikely. It does mean that we no longer live in a world of isolation and isolationism but must live in a world where change is the universal currency. Withdrawal offers little prospect for a good society for a nation as prominent as the United States.

Optimism, more often than not, expresses itself in a state of mind or a persistent attitude toward a particular question. This is true of some of the most profound thinkers discussed in my book *Masters of International Thought: Major Twentieth-Century Theorists and the World Crisis*.[1] In the late fifties and sixties, Father John Courtney Murray was optimistic about the possibilities of a limited nuclear war. It was not that he lacked understanding of international relations as a whole. Indeed, he was one of its most determined students. In his faith in rationalism, he may have overestimated the possibility of reason among nations. So wedded was he to an abstract version of just war that he seized upon limited war, and even limited nuclear war, as the most practical form of just war—a form in which nations would not endanger the world, as in all-out nuclear war. In his use of reason, he succumbed to optimism. Father Murray once referred to me as that "earnest young man" who had doubts about Murray's marriage of reason and optimism. I still have those doubts.

Herbert Butterfield was probably optimistic about "giving peace a chance in the world," although most of his writings were deeply rooted in human tragedy and an understanding of the realities of international relations. Arnold Toynbee was somewhat optimistic about what could be done to bring about a turn in the history of civilizations, where one civilization declined and another took its place. To the end of his career he continued to cling to the hope that Western civilization might avoid the fate of civilizations past. One could say the same about John Herz and the idea of a liberal realism. Fairly often, Herz substituted a good and liberal vision of the world for a realistic conception of what was possible in foreign policy and world affairs.

One could extend this litany of examples showing that optimism of an unthinking kind, or optimism that looks the other way when obstacles impede the achieving of a worthy goal, is a recurrent way

1. Kenneth W. Thompson, *Masters of International Thought: Major Twentieth-Century Theorists and the World Crisis* (Baton Rouge, 1980).

of thinking on the world scene. Optimism that ignores the best available estimates of political realities is like optimism that ignores sometimes useful weather reports predicting tomorrow's weather or conditions next week. We do so because we recognize that the better forecasters understand weather fronts and cloud formations, possible precipitation, wind direction, and highs and lows in the atmosphere that make certain developments more likely than others in emerging weather patterns. The more information, the better their predictions will be. To offer optimism as a substitute for being realistic about foreign policy is to skirt the edges of a know-nothing viewpoint. In other words, to say that what we do know with some degree of probability is irrelevant and need not be heeded, as in evaluating weather conditions, is an attitude of blind optimism.

All this is not to say that realism is irreconcilable with optimism. Many of the leading realists were optimistic at one time or another, in one form or another. Long before the changes had occurred that made the end of the Cold War more likely, Hans J. Morgenthau and George Kennan were optimistic about a possible political settlement between the Soviet Union and the United States. Reinhold Niebuhr saw signs of political change in the Soviet Union when neoconservatives were proclaiming the irreversibility of Communist regimes. Walter Lippmann prophesied that since we had found areas of agreement with Russia in the past, we were likely to do so in the future. These thinkers are examples of guarded optimism. They seek a blending of realism and optimism without abandoning either. Indeed, one can say that realism and optimism are not two opposites on a spectrum but rather two possibilities that sometimes meet. They provide styles of thinking that can sometimes illuminate the unfolding of international relations.

The second attitude or way of thinking about choice involves theory and practice. Theorists often mock the foreign policy decision maker who argues he is free of all assumptions or ideas that guide his actions in foreign policy. They question whether any such decision maker can act in the absence of some conception of what international relations is all about. It would be a mistake to think that to be nontheoretical is to be more realistic. In fact, this is only rarely the case. Theorists are correct in calling attention to the need for controlling ideas that shape theories and principles that can guide people in their actions. One has only to think of other, much less momentous fields, where people make use of the best available concepts and technology. For example, in planning for a major football game, the coach of every intercollegiate team requires detailed analysis, using films and scouting reports, of the strengths and weaknesses of an opponent. Where are the strong points in the rival's game plan, and what type of offensive strategy should the players prepare? How do they strengthen and reinforce their defense? Teams examine all the options as they look at films and charts and make every effort to understand how the other side works. Football strategy has its own "order of battle." It operates within a framework. Thus it seems inconceivable that a leader of a sovereign nation would act in the foreign-relations field without a similar set of underlying assumptions, concepts, and axioms for understanding "the enemy." Assuming such a game plan, the other side must plot out its rival's assumptions, strategy, and strong points. Each creates its framework for analyzing how to defeat the rival team.

For their part, practitioners scorn theorists because they say that their theories have little or nothing to do with practical reality. They offer concepts that could work only if Machiavelli's *fortuna,* or chance, were less of a factor. They would be appropriate if the endless contingencies and accidents of international relations were removed from the picture. But how do you apply a theory when one leader replaces another, as when Yeltsin follows Gorbachev? Where do you find guidelines about the future of Russia today, when most of what we know is bound up with the strategy past leaders have followed? How can we estimate the policies of a nation whose leader clings precariously to power without having the clear support of his parliament?

Thus practitioners have a point about the need to be ever vigilant in dealing with changing realities and not assume that what has happened in the past will happen in the future, especially when the international environment itself is in flux. In some respects, hard-pressed policymakers can only deal case by case with issues as they arise. With each important variable offering new possibilities and new perils and limitations on the ability of nations to influence the course of history, decisions must be made cautiously, one at a time. Policymakers engage in what critics like to call ad hoc policy choices. They move from one crisis to another without pretending to have a global picture covering every aspect of international relations. They are skeptical that anything can replace common sense and good judgment in the choices that have to be made. They break down any problem into components. Whether they like it or not, they are forced to compartmentalize foreign-policy analysis and decision making.

Furthermore, theorists, we are told, ought to "stick to their knitting." They should form a kind of mutual-protection society to defend one another as they seek to put forward new ideals, precepts, and principles, whatever their sphere of endeavor. Theorists have made a contribution—for example, in the history of the American railroad, as Robert Greenfield has shown—when they have sought innovations and new models for the development of the railways or the utility system. Feeling confident about what they have done, theorists then claim the right of being practitioners. In so doing they more often than not founder, because they are ill prepared to deal expeditiously with crises that follow close on the heels of one another in a changing world. Theorists should remain theorists if they are to make contributions. Theorists and practitioners are not interchangeable.

Practitioners, on the other hand, yield to another illusion when they too readily assume they can substitute themselves for theorists. Whatever their experience, whatever their knowledge, however fully they have lived in the world of reality, they lack the capacity to formulate policy designs that might change the process. They provide not a realistic but too often a cynical picture of the world linked with the status quo, questioning whether ideas have any place on the international-relations scene. Practitioners therefore have little to offer in new concepts, new ideas, or new principles that might guide nations to seek a different world.

As with optimism and reality, the schism between theory and practice is not irreconcilable. Theorists and practitioners have been able, at certain periods in history, to work together. When former secretary of state Dean Acheson wrote the introduction to Louis Halle's book,[2] he was correct in pointing out that what Halle, Ken-

2. Louis J. Halle, Jr., *Civilization and Foreign Policy* (New York, 1925).

nan, C. B. Marshall, Nitze, and others were seeking to offer was a relevant body of theory of value both to policymakers and to theorists. They might be able to offer a set of principles providing for viable change but solidly grounded in the bedrock of international-relations practice. Again, as with theorists who depart too widely from reality, a viable theoretical contribution at first seemed unlikely. Acheson himself was skeptical. The notion that fulltime practitioners never deliver applicable principles or theories is, however, belied by a small group who, at various points in their career, have returned to their study or library in search of new ideas that reach beyond the world they have known in experience. Kennan is one example, as is his colleague and friend the late Charles Bohlen. Harold Nicolson was the author of a classic on diplomacy, and Paul H. Nitze is a late-blooming theorist.

One has to say that, although there are tendencies for optimism and realism to break apart and move in opposite directions and similar tendencies for theory and practice to separate and drift in different directions, the history of thought offers examples where this did not occur. Among those who address Third World development, who can match Ambassador Soedjatmoko of Indonesia in relating freedom and development or the role of the intellectual in policymaking? And what of the group of practical scientists and the development of the atomic bomb?

The final way of thinking about choice is through the idea of force versus peace. Force is an ongoing reality in international relations. Violence in the use of force is only one form of its application. Deterrence theory in the Cold War era involves holding back aggression by the threat of overwhelming force as an alternative to force in the form of aggression or violence. This theory introduces a concept that reformers and pacifists choose to overlook. Raymond Aron once wrote that force hangs over the shoulder of every foreign policymaker. It is always there; it may not manifest itself with nations that embrace policies of neutrality, such as Switzerland and Sweden, but even Switzerland has a small but powerful army protecting against invaders, encamped in the mountains and offering security at its borders. Similarly, Sweden has its own forms of influence and power that it seeks to maintain. To exclude as elements of power the preparation for conflict or deterrence against attacks is to be irresponsible. It is closing one's eyes to what every responsible leader knows he must weigh and consider. An axiom of foreign policy is, "Make peace, prepare for war." Among those who talk most strongly about force as a reality, including power, persuasion, and coercion, are E. H. Carr, Hans J. Morgenthau, and Reinhold Niebuhr. To close one's eyes to force is to deny an aspect of the international scene that reflects underlying social forces, social and political realities, and human nature itself.

On the other hand, peace is a condition that nations may pursue through force. Force and peace are not always irreconcilable. "Negotiations based upon strength" was the formula Churchill used to guide his actions in foreign policy. Peace can be pursued in limited social spheres, as in Martin Luther King's nonviolence campaign. Societies with organized systems of law and order are more likely to leave room for pacifists and nonviolent activities as a means to certain ends. It must also be remembered that some of the champions of peace against force show themselves to be among the shrewdest and most canny political leaders, always aware of the reality of power. In modern Indian history, one example is Mahatma Gandhi's struggle with British colonizers.

Thus peace as a simple alternative to force is debatable. Peace, more often than not, is a condition related to preparation for war. Yet certain questions are inescapable—how much preparation? What forms should that preparation take? How should the commitment to force be balanced with the commitment to a more viable economic society or a better social system? Is peace something more than an interval between wars? What are the positive components of peace apart from war? All these issues suggest that peace can never be studied in isolation. Periodically, well-meaning citizens frustrated by a prevailing overemphasis on force have called for the creation of peace academies and peace institutes. Practitioners who are, for the most part, more familiar with the realities of international relations have opposed such proposals. Nonetheless, the two concepts—force and peace—compete now as in the past, and their competition seems likely for the foreseeable future. Force and peace represent two aspects of our nature. One is the strong, bold, and sometimes buccaneering side. It is Machiavelli's *virtù*, or manliness. The other is the quiet, tranquil, peace-loving aspect of human nature that, in spite of everything, pursues peace even in the face of harsh realities.

One way to approach the writings of the eighteen writers on international relations in *Masters of International Thought* or any other group of thinkers would be to consider them in terms of the three categories we have discussed. Optimism and reality, theory and practice, and force and peace form a background against which to explore to what extent any of the thinkers, or all of them or none, emphasize one or the other paired choices. Do they seek rather to blend theory and practice or optimism and reality? Were these writers aware of the multifaceted side of policymaking in the foreign-policy sphere? Did they recognize that no escape is possible from the choices that leaders have to make, often within a narrow framework of action, and without knowing the results that action may bring? Such an inquiry may help in the understanding—perhaps at a deeper level—of the contributions that a thinker has made. If we approach them in the mode of thinking suggested by the twofold division inherent in the three possible conceptual frameworks for organizing ideas, we may enhance our understanding of foreign policy to the level that involves possible linkage between each set of paired ideas. We can only speculate as to the success or failure of those who recognize the dual aspects of human nature—good and evil, patient and impatient, and long-term and short-term commitment. In speculating, however, we can better prepare ourselves for thinking about a future world order.

It seems entirely possible, moreover, that in newspaper articles and journal coverage, wherever ordinary men and women reflect on or observe international relations, they may find it useful to think in terms of force versus peace or optimism versus reality. If they think further, they may find that the paired factors are capable of coexistence. Alternatively, will peace and force always be separate and isolated from one another? Will knowing these tendencies help decision makers do a better job?

These thoughts point up the need for ongoing, persistent, and tireless inquiries into international affairs. The work is never done. The choices that have to be made will confront us as citizen or policymaker. To imagine that we can be wholly free of the need to weigh options is to postulate that a new world has arrived. It may someday come, but it is not yet with us and therefore not deserving of an exclusive focus in our thought. To put forth a conclusion in advance of the next topic, the old and the new world order will always coexist, as will optimism and realism, peace and force, or theory and practice.

ORIENTATION: THE QUEST FOR A NEW WORLD ORDER

We have heard a lot in recent years about a new world order. With the end of the Cold War, the shape of international relations undeniably has been altered. No longer do the two superpowers confront each other, dominating at every point each other's thoughts, calculations, and actions and those of much of the world on every foreign-policy issue. For example, although the United States was criticized for being too restrained in Korea and Vietnam, that restraint reflected the necessity policymakers felt to make decisions with an eye on the Soviet Union and the nuclear threat. To do otherwise would have meant being heedless of threats to human survival. They were being rational and prudent. No nation other than the Soviet Union threatened to destroy the United States. No other nation could wreak universal destruction. The Soviets and the Americans confronted each other along a narrow pathway where compromise and accommodation were difficult, if not impossible. The existence of the two superpowers meant that when people spoke of a new world order, especially after the first five or ten years of the United Nations, they did so in terms of a world order dominated by either the Soviet Union or the United States or both.

The idea of a new world order, however, had been proclaimed more than a quarter century earlier by Woodrow Wilson. Nations no longer gave primacy, he proclaimed, to their own national interest but increasingly viewed the world and their foreign policy as inextricably linked. Any decision that a nation made was bound to affect the fate of all nations scattered around the world. In a sense, Wilson was the first but not the last statesman for a new world order.

Jimmy Carter envisaged a new world order in which human rights would prevail and be practiced throughout the world. Although his vision can now be seen to have been rooted in something more than utopianism, given the growing importance of human rights around the world, he and his immediate associates, Zbigniew

Brzezinski and Cyrus Vance, overestimated the prospect for a truly universal regime of human rights.

At a conference held at the University of Virginia early in the first year of the Carter administration, one of the representatives who was to become assistant secretary of human rights, Pat Derian, argued passionately that it was no longer relevant or necessary to talk of alliances, coalitions, balance of power, spheres of interest, deterrence, and the nation-states of the world. Instead, human rights were transforming rivalries and competition, and a new world order based on human rights was being born in the Carter administration. She also drew the analogy—attractive but misleading—that civil rights and the achievements of a civil-rights revolution within the United States could be replicated on the international scene.

Other presidents had a different picture of a universal global order. In the 1960s, Lyndon Baines Johnson thought of collective security as a realistic possibility. He put forward his views at the outset of the Vietnam War. His secretary of state, Dean Rusk, held much the same viewpoint but on a more realistic and long-term basis. Nations need give less attention to their own national interest but should join with others in protecting common interests in a new world order.

Wilson's slogan that the common purposes of mankind everywhere in the world were replacing national interests has been espoused in varying degrees by other American leaders who have followed one another in the presidency. Franklin Roosevelt's Four Freedoms was a wartime expression of fundamental human rights. The Atlantic Charter embodied concepts of a new world order. All through the history—and especially the early prewar and postwar history—of American foreign policy, the dream expressed as reality of a new world order has found a place in public discourse.

Ironically, the most recent example was the bold vision of President George Bush, whose critics charged he lacked vision. No one asked how someone so lacking in vision could embrace the grandest of all visions—a world united. At the time of the conflict with Iraq and with Saddam Hussein, Bush sought to personalize the conflict with Saddam. The difficulties of this approach became apparent, not immediately, but when the United States had to bargain with the Iraqis, sometimes by force and coercion and, on many occasions, in direct confrontation with officials of Saddam Hussein's regime. Was this the new order or the most recent drama in an old order?

The second feature of Bush's approach was to celebrate the fact that virtually all the nations of the world were joined together in a common enterprise to root out Saddam's aggression. The scene was the Gulf War; the victim was Kuwait. The administration defined the threat by arguing that had the conquest of Kuwait been sustained, Saddam Hussein would have moved on to conquer Saudi Arabia. Very quickly, the forces of aggression would have gained a hold on 40 to 50 percent of the world's oil supply.

George Bush had been ambassador to the United Nations. He had embraced the ideals of the U.N. Charter. He had seen regions in which international cooperation was possible and had hopes that the pattern might be institutionalized. Bush enjoyed remarkable success in speaking to the leaders of international society. Telephone diplomacy came into play, and Bush was more successful than any other modern president since Roosevelt in beguiling, persuading, coercing, arm twisting, and in other ways bringing nations together to form a coalition to support U.S. actions in the Middle East.

Then Bill Clinton came to power. Following his predecessors, he offered yet another vision of a new world order. He envisaged an order in which the primary objectives of the United States would be the promotion and "enlargement" of democracy throughout the world and the creating and buttressing of free-enterprise regimes wherever that was desirable and feasible. The new world order would enlarge the areas of free trade and commerce through agreements such as the General Agreement on Trade and Tariffs (GATT) and the North American Free Trade Agreement (NAFTA). He defended his policies on NAFTA and GATT against the views of some of his party's core constituents, including the labor unions.

Thus, the two most recent administrations have talked in rather sweeping terms about worldwide cooperation. It is noteworthy, however, that the same President Clinton, when forced to assign priority in assistance to a particular nation, decisively chose the former Soviet Union and Russia in particular. The interest of the president in the Ukraine is another example of a national-interest approach. The Ukraine is a large, expansive, and grain-rich country with the third-largest arsenal of nuclear weapons in the world. It is a nation with which a president must deal as others have done before him, but it is secondary to Russia in American foreign-policy priorities.

In *Masters of International Thought,* I discussed several thinkers who address the issue of the old versus the new world order. David Mitrany was the father of an approach called *functionalism.* Functionalism is based on the proposition that nations with projects and activities in social and economic arenas, whose people work together on practical programs such as food production, health, and the building of waterways and irrigation networks, will eventually establish a new world order. Mitrany introduced the idea of the spillover effect. If the leaders of nations could come together and cooperate on social and economic questions, they might move on to discover other areas of cooperation. As they worked together on urgent problems, they would draw closer together and their economic cooperation might spill over into political cooperation. This attitude has had a significant impact on intellectuals and some policymakers concerned with a developing world order.

Many have used Mitrany's ideas about a working-peace system in developing examples and illustrations of world order or in testing the validity of some of his basic propositions. Others have sought to go beyond Mitrany by developing broader concepts and theories such as neofunctionalism, transnationalism, globalism, and interdependence theory. Ernst Haas and the late Karl Deutsch are only two examples of leading scholars who have sought to develop related but not identical theories about international integration. Mitrany's concept of spillover assumes that if individuals of different nationalities work together on common problems, their thinking will become more universalist and less particularist. Unfortunately, Mitrany's prediction has not been borne out by experience. The example he used at the outset of his work was the Tennessee Valley Authority, wherein citizens in the region worked together on projects involving dams, irrigation, and electric power. In crossing local and state boundaries, they developed a regional sense.

Mitrany was an unusual fellow. He never had a tenured university appointment. He was a syndicalist at the beginning of his career. He went on to work as a consultant for corporations at work around the world. He had long, flowing hair and looked like an Old Testament prophet. His impact was in many ways greater than that of fulltime academic scholars. He pressed his claims of an organizing idea for a working-peace system and argued that it could make possible a new world order. Yet the more that nations learned from one another in cooperative fields like health and agriculture, the more national ministers of agriculture and ministers of health claimed credit for new initiatives and advances for their own countries. They maintained that miracle rice or new health-delivery systems that had been the result of cooperative programs across national boundaries were the product of their own national initiatives. In other words, the ministers took credit in the name of their country or their ministry for whatever progress the international body had achieved. National officials were unwilling to give credit to the international cooperative effort.

Nonetheless, the ideas and influence of Mitrany persist. Many are skeptical, but it is significant that the two who wrote introductory pieces to his seminal work, *A Working Peace System: An Argument for the Functional Development of International Organizations,* were Reinhold Niebuhr and Hans J. Morgenthau.[3] Specifically, Morgenthau wrote that if Mitrany's peace plan failed, then peace through any peace system would be unlikely for years to come.

Judge Charles de Visscher put forward a different set of ideas regarding a new world order. He was a senior judge of the International Court of Justice and for a time president of that body. His concept of law was far broader than that of most statesmen or jurists. I visited him in Brussels. His study was the classical European library, with bookshelves stretching from floor to ceiling. Everything about him and his study epitomized the life of the scholar. Somehow he called to mind the French diplomats of the nineteenth and early twentieth centuries. He was a small man, full of energy and compassion, who engaged with anyone who showed interest in his work and especially those who showed signs of developing ideas of their own. I consider him the international legal theorist with the most profound perspective of a new international order. He argued that there could be no legal international order without moral foundations. Undergirding any legal system there must be a normative substructure. Morality is the cornerstone for the building of an effective legal

3. David Mitrany, *A Working Peace System: An Argument for the Functional Development of International Organizations* (London, 1944).

system. Law depends on morality—not morality on law, as Hobbes had argued.

De Visscher was the true scholar, widely read and as much at home in philosophy and history as in the law. His scholarship was enormous. He wrote opinions that are cited to this day in classrooms and at the International Court of Justice as models of objective analysis of international legal problems. His great work is *Theory and Reality in Public International Law.*[4] In it he sets forth his views regarding the international legal system. His book was translated into English by Percy Corbett of Princeton University, and its analysis and concepts were made accessible to those who seek a more fundamental philosophy than a narrow positivism in international law.

De Visscher was hardly optimistic about the early creation of international law. At some time in the future, what he called the "transvaluation of values" might take place. If and when it came about, it would mean that leaders and citizens of participating countries would put first the interests of the world and second, those of their nation as they formulated policy and planned for the future. In that sense, de Visscher was far more exacting and demanding than most world-order thinkers in his vision of a new world system. He saw a new order as possible in some distant future but was never convinced that it would come about in his lifetime. He died in 1973, and no one else has supplied the depth of thought and analysis he introduced into discussions of a new legal world order.

A third person with strong ideas on the new international order was Quincy Wright. He was, as we have seen, the founder of the Chicago School of international relations. More specifically, he represents what many today call a gradualist approach to the new world order. He was intimately familiar with and could discuss many of the territorial disputes and conflicts that had occurred in the nineteenth century. He saw that the role of the balance of power as a factor in world order always had to be kept in mind, even though he believed that the current balance of power was insufficient for the second half of the twentieth century. He recognized the need for alliances among nations. He analyzed with intelligence and wisdom such experiments as the Concert of Europe and the League of Nations.

4. Charles de Visscher, *Theory and Reality in Public International Law*, trans. Percy Corbett (Rev. ed.; Princeton, 1968).

Throughout his career, Wright was both optimist and gradualist in pressing his views on a new international order. He maintained that old practices were probably outdated, but at the same time he continued to discuss alliances and the balance of power.[5] He by no means embraced the view that Secretary of State Cordell Hull expressed on his return from the Moscow conference, when he announced that the United Nations had once and for all supplanted the old diplomacy of the nineteenth and early twentieth centuries. Increasingly in his later years Wright accepted the fact that existing arrangements would continue and were unlikely to change at any time in the foreseeable future. He became less confident concerning the early disappearance of diplomacy's ancient practices.

In the 1930s and 1940s, Wright was preoccupied with *The Study of War*. He came to the conclusion that war was an enduring feature of human history. He wrote less about such topics as the outlawry of war. Nevertheless, he continued to test and explore the prospects for an array of new institutions for peace that were emerging. They included the League of Nations, the United Nations, the Permanent Court of International Justice, the International Court of Justice, and some regional courts and arbitration panels. Wright engaged in many of these undertakings as a consultant and adviser to planners for a new ordering of international institutions. He traveled widely and consulted broadly with those seeking to bring about change. He was optimistic in the sense that he held open the possibility that one such arrangement—perhaps the United Nations—might erode some of the rough edges of unlimited national sovereignty. If nations could be made to work together in the United Nations on projects and programs that were basic to security needs and peace and order, they might then be prepared to accept limitations on absolute natural sovereignty.

Wright was eclectic in his point of view and in his thinking. He drew from many disciplines and the ideas of many nations. Frederick Dunn of Princeton, who led the exodus from Yale to Princeton when the Yale school collapsed in an intramural conflict, had said that the only legitimate approach to international relations was through the study of twenty separate disciplines, each having a part in the study

5. Quincy Wright, *The Study of War*, 2 vols. (Chicago, 1942).

of international relations. If anything, Wright went beyond Dunn's prescription. He consulted with child psychologists, biologists, and anthropologists who had studied conflict. He was indefatigable in looking for new pathways and new routes to peace and understanding. But he never held out much hope that the new world order would come about overnight, nor, on the other hand, did he believe progress was forever foreclosed. He was not opposed to the Committee to Write a World Constitution at the University of Chicago, organized by Mortimer Adler and Robert Hutchins. He never joined, however, and remained apart from most of their activities. He must have found too many of their views impractical and unlikely of achievement. One such view was that because world government was necessary, as Hutchins often said, world government was therefore possible. I doubt strongly that Wright ever went to that length in espousing world government; he had doubts—some of them personal—about certain ideas of the founders of the committee. At the same time, he retained an unquenchable desire to study and encourage new institutions, new arrangements, and new constellations of nations where change might be possible and progress achieved.

These three figures represent points of view that are as relevant in the 1990s as they were in the 1960s to the study of a new world order. Carl Becker's essay "How New Will the Better World Be?" could well describe the core assumptions of at least two of the three who wrote about cooperation.

Arnold J. Toynbee was another thinker who had a continuing interest in a new world order. Toynbee maintained, first, that nations and civilizations came into being in response to major challenges. His concept of the birth of nations and civilizations was based on an idea that he called "challenge and response."[6] When a challenge occurs, a creative minority within some larger group assumes leadership to find new solutions to seemingly intractable problems. This creative minority is, however, unlikely to continue with other new initiatives after its first response or two. Before long, it tends to sit on its oars, retreat from the public arena, and take a generally passive attitude toward the great challenges in its civilization.

Toynbee saw the breakdown of civilizations as occurring when

6. Arnold J. Toynbee, *A Study of History,* 12 vols. (London, 1939–61).

world empires come into being; later, world empires pass into world religions. At one point, he was certain that the final stage in the development of a world civilization is a world religion. He qualified that view, however, and in another connection wrote that the breakdown of nations is a product of war and class. Class within domestic societies, especially class divisions that remained unresolved, can bring down a civilization. The other such force is war. Toynbee was convinced that war is the pattern most likely to assert itself as civilizations become weaker and experience decline. Sometimes empires become overextended and try to conquer too many countries and maintain control over too many states and peoples. Sometimes the decay that brings about their corruption comes from within and involves false leadership. Other times its leaders are good at only one thing. The military, which is good at winning wars, may be poor at negotiating agreements or building peace.

The most significant contribution that Toynbee has made to discussions of the new world order is his argument that at some stage, when it appears that wars are continuing and are simply the prelude to other wars, conflict itself will usher in change. Under the city-state system of earlier civilizations, the Greeks formed temporary unions of city-states. They were organizations that resembled the League of Nations and the United Nations from the standpoint of purpose, although not of structure. One by one these international organizations failed, and in their place the struggle among the city-states continued.

Toynbee saw this struggle in positive terms at the beginning of his history. He praised nationalism and national self-determination, and he came close to saying that nationalism assures political unity and constitutes a necessary form of political religion in the absence of a traditional religion. As he continued to write and study history, however, this view lost much of its appeal. He became more and more fearful of nationalism. Nations have about them a fury that can be destructive and can lead to the ending of any kind of international cooperation. A world order will take their place, but Toynbee was vague in answering the question of how or when. That a philosopher of history made world order part of his history attests to the recurrent character of the idea. That he had difficulty defining or forecasting how or when suggests he had problems similar to those of his three colleagues—David Mitrany, Charles de Visscher, and Quincy Wright.

PHILOSOPHIES: REALISM, LIBERALISM, AND SOCIALISM

Realism is represented by Hans J. Morgenthau, Reinhold Niebuhr, and Herbert Butterfield.[7] I have already discussed Morgenthau and Niebuhr and will return to Herbert Butterfield. Their approach rests on the proposition that world politics is a reflection of human nature. Men act as they do because of human proclivities and tendencies. Certain basic human needs and desires and characteristics of human nature are unlikely to change. The struggle for power reflects the unending search for security that goes on at every level of society. The parent seeks security in relations with the child to assure the maintenance of an authoritative value system and conditions of the status quo. Children assert themselves in a quest for identity in the midst of an ever-changing and uncertain world. They seek to form and define their values or understand and appreciate the values of others. The image of the mother-in-law is symbolic. In some families, rivalry leads to insecurity and competition between the mother-in-law and her child's spouse. The phenomenon reappears in relation among nation-states. Nations in isolation or in association with others seek security through the building up and maintenance of political power, military power, economic power, and social power. They seek prestige as a manifestation of political power. They acquire power, seek to preserve or maintain it, and display it.

The debate over realism has centered on the issue of whether or not this philosophy might lead to the neglect of other goals and values. Is the concern with power likely to diminish an awareness of the importance, say, of freedom or justice in relations among states? Are there purposes and values in society that transcend the acquisition of power? When does the development of power serve as a means to such ends as liberty and justice, and when does it become an end in itself?

These issues and many others have concerned thinkers devoted to a discussion of realism. One who exemplifies the individual re-

7. Hans J. Morgenthau and Kenneth W. Thompson, *Politics Among Nations: The Struggle for Power and Peace,* 6th ed. (New York, 1978).

searcher, the lone scholar at work at his desk, and who, in his mid-nineties, continues to write short essays and letters to editors from his home in Scarsdale, New York, is John H. Herz.[8] Herz was a German refugee scholar who came to this country during World War II. The State Department and the intelligences services called on his knowledge of German culture, the German language, and social and political movements in German society. He was an expert consultant and specialist for several government agencies and served during and after the war. Herz has also had a lifelong interest in comparative government. The largest portion of his writing has been directed to the writing of textbooks in comparative government (one of them with the late Gwendolyn Carter, an American authority on African government and politics) or in separate monographs and papers on particular countries.

Herz taught at the City College of New York. As a professor he was not active in American Political Science Association circles or other organizations or groups. He preferred to follow his own agenda. Before coming to this country, he was an international lawyer of some repute and for a time, therefore, an active member of the American Society of International Law. Again, Herz's research and writing have been that of the solitary scholar at work on his own studies and writings, largely dissociated from large group enterprises by others in his field.

Herz's first book was a study of political realism and political liberalism. Specifically, it examined the compatibility of liberalism and realism. Herz believes that liberalism is the bedrock of Western civilization. It ought not be overlooked in discussions about international relationships or relations between political units of whatever size or character. In this book Herz presses the point that realism, which involves power, requires compromises with the principles of liberalism, which emphasizes freedom and equality. The implementation of realistic ideas is subject to the constraints of liberalism and vice-versa.

Herz asks whether the harsher aspects of realism can be justified given the liberal tradition. It is the humanitarian characteristics of

8. John H. Herz, *Political Realism and Political Idealism: A Study in Theories and Realities* (Chicago, 1951).

American life that especially impress him and lead him to qualify his emphasis on realism.

Liberalism seeks, first, the fulfillment of individual talents and abilities. Liberalism puts stress on change, if not in human nature, at least in certain manifestations of human nature. It sees itself as a philosophy not confined to one or two countries but one that has spread to other countries around the world. Liberalism holds out hope for the universality of democracy.

Herz argues that pure realism is likely to continue as a vantage point at the expense of other enduring values that merit respect and recognition. In his book on political realism and political liberalism, Herz set forth themes that were to be carried forward in all his other works.

Herz was concerned, perhaps more than some fellow realists, with the possibility of change in international society. In midcareer he put stress in his writings on the impact of the nuclear bomb. Nuclear weapons had transformed international relations, but society had not caught up with the fact. Diplomats continued to invoke a philosophy of international relations that had been relevant in a pre-nuclear age but was questionable for a new age.

Herz was ingenious in developing certain operational concepts of international-relations theory. One of them was the idea of the impenetrability of the sovereign state. Later on he was to modify this view, at least in terms of degree. In his first book, he developed the idea that what made relations between states different from relations among individuals was that international relationships involved political units with sovereign status. Sovereign status implied that no nation-state would long remain independent and free if it allowed forces from the outside to penetrate its boundaries. In other words, states must preserve their security if they wish to survive. A state has to protect its citizens if it is to maintain the respect of those who belong to a sovereign state.

Nevertheless, Herz's early work reveals his belief that there was much wisdom in early political realism in the United States. The people he quoted most were Reinhold Niebuhr and Hans J. Morgenthau. He did not set out to overturn in any fundamental way the work they had begun. Still, he was and is a man of vision, some might say more a romantic than a realist. He has sought to identify transforming goals for society. Some of these goals involve the building of a network of relationships between nation-states that places limits on absolute sovereignty.

Herz's early work was nothing so much as a quest for reconciliation between liberalism and realism. It was an attempt to find common ground between concepts of preservation of the state and of individual rights and the protection of individuals in society.

Herz's later writings go on to paint an increasingly apocalyptic picture of the world. Herz sees the world as threatened on all sides by forces that threaten its very survival. These forces include the population explosion, environmental deterioration, and the exploitation and erosion of natural resources beyond what the earth can replace. The world faces multiple threats. The growth in numbers of people in developing societies and nation-states has spiraled out of control. Population growth is capable of destroying viable societies and thwarting the stability of new societies. If too many people are pressed too tightly together in too limited geographic spaces, Herz predicts, catastrophe will ensue.

Closely related to the idea of the population explosion is the imperative of food production. Although Herz has never sought to immerse himself in policies and programs to increase international food production, he has shown a keen awareness that the shortage of basic food crops poses a threat of world hunger and famine. In his opinion, Americans consume too much and produce too little. He finds this true with regard to both agriculture and the development of the industrial plant. He believes that Malthus' prophecy of overpopulation was staved off in past generations by famine and disease but has reemerged as a grave threat to survivability. What has happened since World War II confirms Herz's prophecy that a crisis exists in the food-population equation and that basic human needs extend beyond the capability of available agencies and institutions.

Herz has never been specific about ways of dealing with the crisis. He has had little to say about what the U.N. Food and Agriculture Organization ought to do, or what role private organizations seeking to conquer world hunger should play, or what the responsibility of national government or international organizations ought to be. He has discussed the problem without prescribing remedies or considering ways for bringing about improvement. His purpose has been to urge the country's leadership to focus attention on these sectors. From time to time he still issues warnings to a society under siege.

Herz put forward another novel concept—that our present dire situation might prove so overwhelming that rather than thinking of reforms or new institutions and new approaches, we ought to be thinking about what route the individual can follow when the food supply drops off or environmental destruction becomes too great. He introduced the idea of an ethic of "exit from the world." His argument is that we should think more about how to free ourselves from human limitations and the restrictions of the present world. We ought to give attention to such ideas as *triage* (although he has never used that word) to rescue societies, for example, caught up in human devastation from famine. We ought to broaden our horizons to include planetary thinking.

This brief review is intended to provide a portrait of a serious thinker struggling to define the basic operating principles of international relations—if not the laws of politics set forth by the realists. Herz's passion is defending liberal values. Liberal values come into play in calculations of just-war theory—in limiting the destructive military power to be deployed to the threat against which it is being applied. These values also illuminate such problems as the poisoning of the environment and the search for a balance in the food and population equation.

The socialist philosophy and viewpoint is a perspective that E. H. Carr embraced more strikingly than any other modern international theorist. Carr was often attacked for his Marxist worldview. He worked for the intelligence services in the British government during World War II, and for a time thereafter he continued his association with government. His background was entirely different from that of the more privileged class of Englishmen such as Arnold Toynbee. He had risen through the ranks of voluntary discussion groups involving lower- and lower-middle-class people. For a time Carr maintained his interest in these groups, but they lacked the prestige of Chatham House, where Toynbee and Martin Wight held forth.

Carr's most formidable work is his history of the Bolshevik revolution and of the changes taking place in the Soviet Union. He went further in his overall socialist perspective, however. The crisis leading up to World War II, Carr maintained, could have been prevented had there been sufficient economic planning, social forecasting, and looking ahead, particularly on the part of the British and French. Germany and Italy achieved dramatic economic progress because they turned to the state to engineer programs of economic and social planning based on the tenets of socialism. Mussolini made the trains run on time. Hitler brought Germany's catastrophic inflation under control. Morgenthau used to talk of his mother and neighbor women going to market to shop with a baby carriage full of deutsche marks. Inflation was rampant and the currency declined on the way to market. Carr seeks to offer remedies for such problems.

Carr insisted that Germany and the Soviet Union in particular and Italy in certain limited respects had made significant headway through foresight in social and economic planning. They had looked ahead and had abandoned all-out free enterprise. They substituted socialist planning. The same was true of Mussolini and would be true of other socialist states. According to Carr, Britain and France had lagged behind because they had clung to outmoded and obsolete economic and social doctrines.

At the same time, Carr was a realist. He pointed out that realism always moves through certain well-defined stages in its development. In the beginning, a vision, a human need, or a utopia motivates social planning and social action; the need for a bridge or a harbor comes before the development of the science of engineering. Sick people, disease, and epidemics stimulate the development of the medical sciences. Realism is a response to actual social and world problems that were earlier identified. Realists who respond see themselves as substituting a more practical and pragmatic approach to urgent problems, contrasted with a wholly utopian plan. Carr was especially critical of some international-assistance agencies. One that he frequently denounced he called "Sunfed." He advised his students to stay away from such multilateral-assistance agencies because they gave little promise of dealing successfully with the pressing problems of the age.

In his writings on the Bolshevik revolution, Carr concentrated on the constitutional and political realities that were being gradually put into practice and proclaimed by Bolshevik leaders. By state proclamations and the promises of Communist leaders, the Soviet Union was advancing along a similar path to that of Germany and Italy. If this should continue, Carr believed that the Soviet republics would move into an era of harmony, self-sufficiency, and economic development. New political institutions would emerge from the social and economic structures that the planning agencies had institutionalized.

This view of the social order and of the merging of socialized institutions with free enterprise dominated Carr's thought and made him reluctant to accept any of the more limited and incremental advances taking place in Britain and France. He underestimated the emerging strength of those countries and, to some extent, of the United States, although he wrote less about the weaknesses of the West's emerging superpower. He overestimated the capacity of a socialist order to fashion solutions to intractable problems and put them into effect. Toward the end of his life, he said that if he were to rewrite his history of Bolshevism and some of his lesser works on the Soviet Union, he would pay more attention to the practice of deliberate torture and cruelty and the sacrifice of human lives in the name of so-called Communist utopias. He acknowledged he had been too quick to conclude that Soviet constitutional principles were being implemented in communist policy.

One can argue that the two alternatives—liberalism and socialism—can be linked and related in a discussion of realism. Realism attempts to describe the means required to arrive at certain ends. It seeks to make clear the constraints imposed by human nature. It undertakes to suggest the limits of institutions and laws. The area within which liberalism and socialism may have their greatest impact is in new visions for the future. These visions, however, often harden into rigid dogmas and ideologies, even though they appear, especially in the beginning, to offer broad outlines of what men and women strive for in the development of their own countries.

Liberalism and socialism have their own intellectual foundations. Liberalism in its pragmatic forms has been tried and tested. It has been partially successful in the solution of certain problems in society but has failed in other respects. Liberalism has tended to underestimate the influence of the great collectivities that organize themselves and seek political power in society: nation-states, great corporations, and alliances and coalitions.

Liberalism seeks to transplant from the domestic realm principles that claim applicability around the world. An example is projecting the lessons of civil rights in the worldwide struggle for human rights. Statesmen from Franklin D. Roosevelt to Bill Clinton have led the charge. Liberalism's point of view and its vantage point for viewing history is from the top down; ironically, it is similar to conservatism in this regard, whereas realists look at the political process from the ground level up. Some significant distinctions can be made between the two approaches, yet there are also points of congruence, including an emphasis on the importance of setting priorities and goals.

Socialism is the doctrine that came to dominate social and political thinking for a time after World War I. It played a part in social thinking within the United States. Walter Lippmann and other intellectuals were socialists or pseudosocialists in their outlook when they founded the *New Republic*. Europe witnessed a resurgence of socialist and social-democratic thinking after World War II. Most labor parties tend to be socialist.

Students of Reinhold Niebuhr point to the interplay between his writings and the unsettling events that were occurring all around him. For instance, the alternative to Marxism and socialism, as we have seen, was the idea of liberalism. Liberalism had provided Reinhold Niebuhr with a philosophical home when he was a minister in a small Detroit church whose membership and support increased exponentially during his pastorate. Niebuhr was sustained by a body of liberal beliefs that he was in the process of continually reexamining.

After a time, Niebuhr concluded that liberalism itself is subject to criticism because of several illusions. One is the liberal assumption that education of the individual is an answer to most of the nation's problems. If the education of individuals could be achieved, that would ensure the entire society's good health. Niebuhr concluded that this is incorrect. More often, the great collectivities and political alliances accumulate political power in society and determine its fate. Niebuhr was skeptical of the slogan that education can save us; yet he acknowledged that education can do many things. It prepares the human spirit for a happier and more fulfilling life. It broadens our horizons. It adds to imagination and understanding as well as prepares us for a fruitful career. It provides opportunities for advancement. But Niebuhr insisted that the belief that education can solve all the problems of a weakened economy is incorrect because in and of itself, the economy yields primarily to forces of the market, political pressures, coercion, the invoking of government authority, and the influence of special-interest groups. Moreover, education often seems remote from the lives of people struggling with low incomes or inadequate housing, or against social and economic forces beyond their control.

It was not that Niebuhr felt that the philosophies of liberalism and education were wrong; it was simply that they were insufficient. Education alone cannot solve all of society's problems. Leadership— the capacity to mobilize people, to build coalitions, and to organize resistance to the forces of special privilege—can be more important than education for a good society. Leadership and social action involve a knowledge of politics. Niebuhr was prepared to say that politics was essential for the health and well-being of society, sometimes more than education.

Niebuhr also questioned the liberal idea that education is a universal force. He argued that education is linked to the culture of the people and that it arises in the social and political context of a society. It is different from country to country and responsive to a variety of human needs. For some individuals, vocational education is more important than a broad liberal education. Basic science merits society's respect but so do various forms of applied science. In Western society, education has had the effect of strengthening and reinforcing tradition and culture; but in Third World cultures, education oftentimes destroys indigenous traditions and erodes native values while offering modernizing principles in return. Who is to say what the tradeoff should be?

At one point Niebuhr rejected outright the Marxist criticism of liberalism. He declared that the Marxist solution was worse than the flawed system it sought to replace. Marxism was tyrannical. Marxism involved the exploitation of large groups for the benefit of smaller groups. As we know, Stalin was once asked by Lady Astor why he participated in the killing of five million *kulaks,* and he responded by asking her how many people were killed on the highways of England each year. When she answered with a very large figure, Stalin replied, "And to what end?" For Stalin, the noble objectives of communism—economic progress and agricultural reform—demanded the elimination of obstructionist *kulaks.* By comparison, what worthy end was served by the killing of thousands of people in accidents on the highways and in the streets of London? In effect, he argued that a genuine social and economic purpose lay behind the ruthless acts and terrible brutality of the Soviet regime, whereas the killing of people on the streets of London and on highways was random, arbitrary, aimless, and futile. It could not be justified by any rational objective.

Niebuhr spoke out on a range of issues in the social and international order of the 1930s. Prior to World War II, two of the problems that occupied much of his attention were the economy and the prospects for a second world war. Most of his writing touched upon or came into focus on these two questions. He proposed changes, ways of dealing with problems, ideas, and modifications that might come from other countries. He went to the Soviet Union with Sydney and Beatrice Webb, the English socialists, to assess and judge what the Soviet Union had to offer. That experience was almost totally disillusioning to Niebuhr, because he came back convinced that the greatest evil in the Soviet Union came from its merging of political and economic power. At least within a free-market economy, the forces of the economy and the free-market system were balanced by the regulatory and supervisory authority of government. In the United States, we have a checks-and-balances system. We have political parties that vie with one another, representing to the voters their respective viewpoints and ideas. In the Soviet Union, the government and the economy were united under a single, all-controlling political system that made all decisions for the people. Niebuhr concluded that the combining of politics and economics was a far more serious threat to the survival of a legitimate society than was communism as a political religion in the world.

What was threatening, then, was not the construction of a political religion that offered an alternative to the traditional religions of the Soviet Union. The greater threat was the fact that any act within the society and beyond was justified by what Niebuhr called the Soviet or Communist utopia. Communism was a single goal and single vision of what was good for the Soviet Union. All of the legitimizing elements of communism were linked together and absorbed in the Soviet utopia, and that utopia led Soviet and Communist leaders to justify acts of violence, cruelty, brutality, and destruction of human life carried out in its behalf. The Lady Astor example is to the point: what Stalin meant was that it was no great loss to kill five million Soviet farmers in the name of Soviet reform because that reform was so pure and noble in its aims and intention that anything occurring under its mantle was totally justified. The end justified the means. The end of Soviet society as promised by Marxist scientific history was beyond questioning or debate. Self-criticism and self-examination aside, whatever Soviet leaders did could find justification in the utopia.

Because of his energy, personality, and character, Niebuhr contended tirelessly with all these forces. Niebuhr could not remove himself from the battle. He preached as a believer in Christianity and the idea of a transcendent religion. He once made the comment that he could not look back to a time in his life when he had any serious doubt about the existence of God. He never joined the "God is dead" movement. He never gave religion second place, as in some forms of liberal Protestantism. Instead, he held to the view that religion must continuously renew, legitimize, and recommit itself and demonstrate its relevance to the great human problems.

At each point along the way, it would have been easier for Niebuhr not to have taken stands on crucial issues. His church in Detroit, which soon became a famous Protestant parish and which led to his appointment as Briggs Professor at Union Theological Seminary in New York, is a case in point. The membership core and major supporters were people like Henry Ford, industrialists, and businessmen. They were people who were hungry for praise and justification of the American economy as it operated and of free markets.

It was not, however, the big contributors or the supporters of the industrial class as a whole to whom Niebuhr turned with greatest sympathy. He became instead the defender of the little people—the shopkeepers, the postmen, and the workers. When the workers went on strike and were in turn attacked and struck down with great cruelty by Henry Ford and his associates, Niebuhr aligned himself with the workers. Yet, almost in spite of themselves and because of the sheer force of Niebuhr's intellect and his incorruptible character, business leaders remained to listen. They did not abandon him but continued to build his congregation into a pillar of spiritual strength in the Detroit area.

After moving to New York, Niebuhr quickly found himself in a larger world. He ran for Congress once and was not successful. I never heard him discuss the contest, except to say he was not cut out for politics. He was not a party-line thinker or strict politician in any sense of the word. He was more often a member of the New York Liberal party than of the Democrats or Republicans. As a practical politician, Niebuhr had no chance in the society in which he labored and worked. He laughed when someone asked to submit his name for the presidency of Yale. But it was as a thinker who asked the hard questions and challenged others to examine their assumptions that Niebuhr led people to weigh and consider issues that the popular media or interest groups were not addressing.

Along the way, he founded three journals and pioneered with networking in advance of his time. The first journal, *Radical Religion,* represented a phase in his life when he was critical of liberalism for its extreme individualism. Next, he founded *Christianity and Society,* and finally, *Christianity and Crisis.* The most significant attribute of them all, but particularly *Christianity and Crisis,* was Niebuhr's success in recruiting the best minds here and abroad— especially in Europe—to write articles, review books, and explain issues. The little journal became one of the most widely read and quoted little journals in the nation. Secular and religious readers alike hastened to open the next issue. *Christianity and Crisis* only recently closed its doors, but without Niebuhr it had lost some of its intellectual and moral reach. Niebuhr tried to provide moral and political leadership through each of the small, low-cost magazines he founded. He also sought to lead more directly through tying these little magazines to periodic conferences for people from all denominations who came together and discussed political and social issues. Without advertising it as such, his was an adventure in ecumenism.

Niebuhr extended his outreach even further by participating as "an intellectual adviser and gadfly," in his words, in public-policy groups. For example, along with Hubert H. Humphrey, Elmer R. Davis, and Edward R. Murrow, he was an active member of the Americans for Democratic Action. The strength of the ADA in the 1950s and its vitality reflected the quality of its leaders, above all Niebuhr. Their conferences were gatherings in which intellectuals educated themselves in things political. I attended one of the sessions where, early in debates about the city, public housing was discussed, and Hubert Humphrey took part in the debate. The discussion fore-shadowed what happened to Humphrey over Vietnam, in the 1968 presidential race. Because the bulk of ADA members at the meeting (who were part of a liberal but not extreme left group) insisted there should be no support for public housing unless it made provision for minority housing, a public-housing measure was defeated. Hubert Humphrey and Niebuhr, to a lesser extent, were in the minority. They argued that by waiting for a perfect solution or the ideal public housing plan, there might be no public housing at all. The only chance for public housing would be through a bill enacted by com-promise and give and take. It had to be accepted that sometimes you only get half a loaf. You wouldn't get all that you wanted in public housing, but at least you could get homes where people could live, people who were the disadvantaged and homeless in the big cities. Niebuhr thought some housing was a step forward. Humphrey also defended the measure, but he received catcalls and hisses from the participants. As I remember, he lost the vote.

The ADA experiment represented an attempt by people like Humphrey and Niebuhr to take part in political debate, but not as ideologues or partisan political leaders. With the possible exception of John F. Kennedy's presidential campaign, I cannot remember when Niebuhr either praised effusively or criticized harshly candi-dates for office—quite a contrast to the Falwells and the Robertsons of our day or even the Ralph Reeds or Yale's religious right. The one exception was John F. Kennedy, and for months Niebuhr hesitated to endorse Kennedy in the contest with Nixon. His hesitation was not due to a high opinion of Nixon. Indeed, he saw little good in Nixon. If anything, he underestimated Nixon's more positive quali-ties, for example, in foreign policy. He was put off by Kennedy's personal life, however, and by his father's heavyhanded intervention in the political process. Thus, for a time he refused to join Arthur Schlesinger, Jr., James MacGregor Burns, and other good friends in supporting Kennedy. He finally agreed to endorse him but without enthusiasm and mainly because of his opposition to Nixon. Later, he praised Kennedy for his statesmanship in civil rights and foreign pol-icy and, as so often was the case, displayed "the courage to change."

These attitudes and this kind of approach set Niebuhr apart. He was not the spokesman for the "moral majority," or any kind of majority that justified itself in the name of religion or self-appointed virtue. He said that religion was sometimes harmful to the political process and to the quality of political participation. He used to say there is religion for the good man and religion for the bad man. The bad man exploits religion and uses it as a fig leaf to conceal his selfish acts. Niebuhr was never convinced that anyone could bring religion directly into the political arena and draw from it readymade answers for the conduct of government along more virtuous lines. He often talked of those who lobby for special favors in the courts of the Almighty on behalf of their own special interests. He had in mind religious people who were forever claiming that they deserved the public's support because they were so virtuous or so religious.

What we have witnessed in the United States in the last two decades is the advancement of narrowly partisan political interests by sectarians invoking religion. All this is utterly alien to what Niebuhr had in mind. He understood that in politics as in life, with hard choices following one another in rapid succession, we seldom have simple choices between good and evil. More often, the choice is between lesser evils or relative goods. Actions that are good in only a qualified sense sometimes deserve public support, even though the public would prefer black-and-white answers.

Niebuhr sought to educate church people in the dynamics of practical politics, not to preach partisan politics. He said politics was a terribly complex arena in which decisions should be made in light of the choices and the probable consequences. In this, he was influenced by Max Weber, who spoke about the ethics of intention and the ethics of consequences. Niebuhr never thought of exhausting his view of politics by speaking only of consequences as alone determinative of the good, but he felt that consequences were a vital aspect of political ethics often overlooked, especially by those who talked endlessly about their own righteousness and the good. We often fail to think ahead and measure the consequences of our favorite policies in politics as we do in life's decisions. Consequences are more important at the center of a system of political ethics than ideologies that present one messianic political creed or one political system or a single public policy as everywhere and forever superior.

Niebuhr's influence was closely bound up with his skills and fervor as a communicator. Alan Paton called him the greatest orator of the century. *Cry the Beloved Country* was Paton's powerful work on the immorality of race relations in South Africa. He stated that of all the social reformers, all the prophets and political and religious leaders in his time, no one compared with Niebuhr as a public speaker. Looking down from the pulpit or speaker's podium, Niebuhr seemed to be an inspired prophet giving birth to ideas as he stood before an audience. He spoke about fundamental issues to which he had given deep thought or on which he had written or was continuously re-examining and reconsidering. As he spoke, it was as though he was discovering ideas afresh. He gave the impression that what he was presenting came from the core of his being, came about as a result of a struggle and represented his most valiant attempt—at least to that point—to help others know what he was himself struggling to understand. He spoke of moral dilemmas, the human predicament, crises in the world, and evil that would never be wholly extinguished. *Time* magazine, in listing the intellectual and political giants of twentieth-century America, chose Niebuhr as the one and only theologian deserving of inclusion.

Thus his ability as a speaker had a far-reaching impact. Few American historians have matched him in articulating a philosophy. Some people said it was easier to follow Niebuhr as a speaker than as a writer. His writing sometimes was too complex and dialectical for the untrained person. Following his speaking could also be a challenge. After Niebuhr had suffered two damaging strokes, friends wryly remarked that his illness, strangly enough, was a blessing in disguise because an audience could more easily follow him than when he was in full strength.

Niebuhr also had an uncanny ability to work through a problem. Once I asked him how he had mastered the art of speaking so that he captured listeners' interest and attention. He answered, "Oh, I just open my mouth and let the words come out." That was a quip and a turn of phrase. But it was not the way Niebuhr went about grappling with and understanding issues. He prepared for weeks and months for every major lecture and most especially for every major sermon, whether at Union Theological Seminary in New York, Harvard, Chicago, or Yale. He was an itinerant Sunday preacher, a kind of modern circuit rider. I once heard Niebuhr in an informal discussion group speaking about the role of psychology in politics. He hadn't sharpened or refined his thoughts, even though there were flashes of sheer brilliance and profound insight. He called up other viewpoints and approaches, usually to criticize them. In this setting, a certain lack of coherence characterized what he said.

When he prepared for a Harvard or a Union Theological sermon, he brought it into being over time. As I remember it, he devoted much of the autumn to preparing for a sermon in the late fall. When he engaged in serious discourse, using insights and citations from the world's great thinkers, the resulting text was no hasty improvisation, even though it may have appeared he was throwing off ideas. He had given the subject sustained thought, even though ideas seemed to come easily.

Yet society imagines that speakers and performers excel at no great price. Niebuhr paid for his intense concentration, perhaps in the end with his life. He worked tirelessly and tested his ideas with friends, faculty, and students. For example, he held regular Wednesday evening discussions with faculty and graduate students from Columbia University, Jewish Theological Seminary, and Union Theological Seminary. He reached out in an organized way, with thoroughness and resolve. Yet he was above all and in the most profound sense a pastor. He sought better ways to communicate not only on religion and politics but with society at large.

The other thing he did that enabled him to hone his foreign-policy insights was to participate and join study groups in organizations such as the New York Council on Foreign Relations. He commented to friends on the ideas John J. McCloy, Averell Harriman, George Kennan, Charles Bohlen, and others put forward at the Council. Thus his views on foreign policy were not simply the product of abstract philosophy or religious writings justifying a certain sectarian point of view. Instead, they were the product of rigorous examination of the most difficult issues that confronted leaders in politics and international relations. Whatever he said or wrote merited attention.

It is well to remember that even as remarkable a man as Reinhold Niebuhr achieved what he did because of concentration. He seldom let loose of a problem with which he was struggling. Shortly before his death, Morgenthau, my son Ken, and I went to see him. He was able to communicate only with the greatest difficulty. A nurse rolled him in a wheelchair into the living room of his Stockbridge, Massachusetts, home. We talked briefly before he went back to bed. Then each in turn, Morgenthau and I went to his bedroom and held his hand and talked with him gently about his illness and our love and respect for him. Earlier, however, when he had come out of his sickroom, the first thing he had wanted to talk about was the current crisis in the Middle East. Even in very poor health, he struggled to comprehend and interpret the issues of the day. He rarely shot from the hip. He didn't let some simple ideological position determine what he had to say. He could never be classified as wholly a conservative or a liberal because depending on the circumstances his views could be either conservative or liberal or some combination of the two. If he held Marxist beliefs, it was for the briefest period. He dealt with problems where he found them and on the merits. The problem shaped his approach and his responses. He thought for himself, and he was above all a Christian realist.

Niebuhr's influence had a human side that must be considered in evaluating his impact. He had a way of extending interest and encouragement to almost everyone he met who shared a serious interest in politics and religion.[9] This was true in my case, and a personal experience may illustrate it for readers.

In the late 1940s I took part in a seminar at the University of Chicago sponsored by the Norman Waite Harris Foundation. The subject was Germany and Europe after World War II. The participants included German scholars who came as refugees to the United States from Europe. Others were German-Americans and French-Americans who had been in this country for longer periods. They presented papers or were major discussants of papers and presentations. After the debates had gone on for the better part of a morning or afternoon, graduate students were invited to ask questions or make comments. It was a unique experience. It provided us with a sense of involvement. We students sat in a circle on the periphery of a large table around which the speakers and discussants faced one another. The purpose of our presence was to raise questions that had not yet been addressed.

I asked a question that had to do with the possibility of Soviet-

9. Reinhold Niebuhr, *The Irony of American History* (New York, 1952).

American negotiations on the future of Germany. I suggested that Germany remained pivotal to any reduction of tensions in the heart of Europe. Walter Lippmann, George Kennan, and Hans Morgenthau had each proposed that soundings be taken on such questions as the boundaries between Germany and the Soviet Union or other issues of strategic and territorial importance. At the time there was skepticism and prejudice in the West against high-level discussions. Governments insisted that unless secretaries of state and foreign ministers laid the groundwork through preparations at their level, little or nothing would be accomplished at the summit. Others, such as Secretary of State Dean Acheson, insisted we must negotiate from "situations of strength." Some who opposed discussions with the Soviet Union on the question of Germany expressed fear that the Soviets would outnegotiate us or that we might stumble into another world war, much in the same manner as World War I and II had begun.

Niebuhr responded to my question, expressing doubt that the time was ripe for such an approach, and silence followed. I restated my question and pushed him a bit on his answer. He responded in kind and the meeting ended. As we were leaving the room, he was standing at the door and asked my name and my position. I had left the University of Chicago to teach at Northwestern University. Years later, Niebuhr was invited to give a series of endowed lectures at Northwestern. One morning I got a call saying that he would like to talk with me and had been asking where he could find me. Eventually, we met and spent the better part of a morning discussing common concerns and issues. I still cherish that experience.

I mention my experience not to exaggerate the extent of my personal relations with Niebuhr or the benefits I extracted from that relationship. Rather, my personal story illustrates Niebuhr's unflagging interest in younger people and his wish to maintain a continuing association with them. His interest was fruitful for me, and we began a long correspondence. He made a special effort; he went so far as to inquire of the president of the university where he could find Kenneth Thompson. It was in his makeup that he sought out young minds that were struggling for understanding.

Niebuhr's association with other scholars is illustrated even more significantly in the case of four figures who shared some of his interest in politics and religion: Herbert Butterfield, Martin Wight, Arnold Toynbee, and John Courtney Murray. Niebuhr's relationship with Butterfield was sparked by discussion at a professional meeting. Butterfield had given a paper and made some proposals about the ending of the Cold War and the reduction of tensions, and Niebuhr had responded. During the Cold War, Butterfield often spoke of the need "to take a chance for peace." He believed in diplomacy and was convinced that no reasonable relationship between the Soviet Union and the United States was possible without improved personal contacts. As a young student, Butterfield had been touted as one of the potential greats in British history. His mentor was Harold Temperley, one of the towering figures in British historical studies. Temperley wanted Butterfield to follow the traditional course of studies that most European and British historians and scholars pursued. Butterfield, however, had enjoyed an early religious upbringing that left a permanent imprint on his goals and values. His father was an itinerant minister of sorts and wanted Herbert to be a minister as well. Butterfield demurred and said he lacked talent for the ministry and the kind of public speaking it required. He did, however, set out on a historian's odyssey that had a religious and philosophical dimension. He wrote a book on the novel as history, pointing out the importance of superior writing. He gave a series of endowed lectures, the most famous being the Gifford Lectures. He combined an interest in Western history with an interest in China, science, and political leadership in China. All this was part of his effort to understand the world and to fit the world into the mold of history that he was shaping and delineating.

Butterfield had formed an independent study committee in Britain, the British Committee on the Theory of International Relations. He asked Martin Wight to be cochairman. In spelling out the role of the committee, Butterfield noted that it was more interested in history than in game theory, in political philosophy than analytic philosophy. The British had more to contribute with their institutional interests and the study of norms than in international law or behavioral studies.

In the last years of Butterfield's life, he pulled together his correspondence and papers, and sent some of them to me for safekeeping and to the Miller Center. He made progress in answering the question of where history began. In what was the principal theme of his Gifford Lectures he sought to understand the origins of history. He also dealt with more contemporary topics in a series of books and writings. In *Origins of Science* he attempted to look at the beginnings of science and its development from a historian's standpoint.[10] He undertook to explore the roots of every subject that he addressed but he also insisted that in such an exploration, the story must be told with accuracy and good judgment. He emphasized the importance of the texture of history and wrote of certain norms whose application was unchanging and others that were more flexible and could bend with events.

Many others were influenced by Niebuhr's thought. Perhaps the most notable was Father John Courtney Murray, who was a professor at Woodstock College and editor of several Catholic journals. He thought and wrote almost exclusively within the Catholic tradition.

Father Murray was a lifelong student of just-war theory, and he invoked many of its principles in his discussions of war.[11] War must be authorized by a recognized and competent authority. It must involve actions proportionate to the evil that is being resisted or opposed. If the intervention goes beyond prudent measures in the conduct of a just war, it is no longer just. In particular, the uses of force and weaponry in a just war must be proportionate to the evil that is being opposed. In these terms, Murray pursued what Aristotle had begun and Thomas Aquinas had continued, namely, the historic tradition of just war. He brought it up to date and argued that it must be applied in the relationships of the superpowers.

As with Niebuhr, Murray was a person who never shrank from conflict. He endorsed policies of limited nuclear war. He lived with the illusion that nuclear war could be limited. Niebuhr espoused the opposite view—that once a nuclear conflict broke out no limitations were possible. When a nation became a party to a limited nuclear war using tactical nuclear weapons, there was no way to contain it or resist escalation. Henry Kissinger came to a similar conclusion when he revised the thesis of his book on nuclear weapons and foreign policy.

10. Herbert Butterfield, *The Origins of Science* (London, 1949). See also Herbert Butterfield and Martin Wight, eds., *Diplomatic Investigations: Essays in the Theory of International Relations* (London, 1966).

11. John Courtney Murray, *Morality and Modern War* (New York, 1959).

Today, almost all observers doubt that nuclear war can be contained or limited.

Father Murray was a powerful speaker, and with certain audiences he may even have outdone Niebuhr. At six feet four inches tall, he was the picture of the avenging angel, a priest who walked in flowing gowns and became excited when others presented viewpoints that he considered misplaced and ill directed. He never developed his writings into a major corpus. He was the chief draftsman and the champion in Vatican II of the articles on the separation of church and state. He was wary of too much concentration of power. He and Niebuhr engaged in a series of debates on ethics and foreign policy that those who heard them never forgot.

The final writer is Martin Wight. Wight was at one time a staunch British pacifist working at a pacifist bookstore. He saw it as a grievous human error to have joined in such a conflict as World War II. Wight, however, was too much the student of the lessons of history in international relations to desist from continually reexamining his pacifist viewpoint. He modified it and, in fact, wrote a short book, *Power Politics,* that was for many years the model summary volume on the nature of international politics.[12] It was a one-hundred-page volume, and not until several of Wight's students collected their notes of his lectures, revised the text, and added to its pages did it become a full-fledged study. To a considerable degree, Wight's influence stemmed from the fact that he was a great teacher. He was the professor of Hedley Bull, and with his book *The Anarchic Society* the latter continued in the tradition Wight had established. They both divided international-relations thinking into three schools: the Kantian or revolutionary viewpoint; a centrist perspective identified with Grotius and international law; and a realist mode of thought as represented by Machiavelli, although Wight also mentioned Hobbes in this connection.

Thus realism, liberalism, and socialism found expression in some of the major thinkers in contemporary international relations. It is noteworthy that a study of their writings suggests a crossing over from one to another of these approaches. Herz defended both traditional realism and liberalism. Niebuhr embraced liberalism early in

12. Martin Wight, *Power Politics,* ed. Hedley Bull and Carsten Holbraad (New York, 1978).

his career but at the end described himself as a Burkean conservative and Christian realist. Carr was both a liberal and a socialist, and Butterfield pursued the study of Whig history as a Christian realist. Wight was a liberal pacifist who came to recognize the demands of realism in foreign and military policy. Murray was a natural-law theologian who in his time defended limited nuclear war. Indeed, our greatest interpreters of international relations have moved strongly across the landscape of realism, liberalism, and socialism. Morgenthau combined realism with economic thinking. He assumed the need for a mixed economy. Others, including Niebuhr, challenged class theory in sociology. The history of thought is a chronicle of the interrelation of multiple intellectual trends of thought by minds that have struggled to find meaning in the complexities of politics and the enduring qualities of human nature.

IV

UNRESOLVED ISSUES

SYSTEMATIC THINKING OR SYSTEMS THEORY

If we seek to characterize the present period in international thinking, one distinguishing characteristic is the intellectual ferment engendered by what might be called the fourth great debate. The first great debate was a controversy in the 1950s over certain realist ideas challenged by idealists as running counter to the American tradition. The idealists spoke out for a tradition of exceptionalism, or the idea that the United States was unique among nation-states. The second great debate engaged the proponents of the classical versus the so-called scientific approach. The third debate was a contest between the interdependency and nation-centered schools of thought. Today, the defenders of systemic theory and of systematic thinking confront each other. Before we examine the current debate, it may be useful to review some of the issues raised in the earlier great debates.

Realism and the Coordinate State

The first great debate was advertised, at least by some, as a controversy between the advocates of the coordinate state and those of the balance of power. It is more accurately described as a debate between American exceptionalism and the idea of the national interest. A rather combative idealist who was a professor of history at Columbia University, Frank Tannenbaum, argued that the debate was precipitated by those who urged Americans to abandon their humanitarian traditions and adopt power politics as the basis for American foreign policy. Ironically, Tannenbaum himself had earlier written an article defending the balance of power. He found that the doctrine was gleefully amoral and embraced Machiavelli as its teacher. It was contemptuous of "the simple beliefs of honest men," ridiculed sentimentalism, and attacked democracy as an obstacle to diplomacy. It had criticism for the greatest of American presidents, including Jefferson, John Quincy Adams, Woodrow Wilson, and Franklin D. Roosevelt. Its heroes were Richelieu, Clemenceau, and Bismarck. Worst of all, this "dreadful doctrine" had won the support of teachers and scholars at leading universities. It threatened to throw law and morality out the window, and to what end? It would promote the practice of secret diplomacy from one war to the next. It would destroy international goodwill, friendship among nations, the security of treaties, respect for international law, and human rights.

The heart of the matter was the source of these ideas. The two approaches have opposing views of the nature of man and of international institutions. The balance of power approach derives its precepts from the European nation-state system, whereas the other philosophy takes inspiration from the American federal system, the Organization of American States (OAS), the British Commonwealth of Nations, and the federative system of Switzerland. The idea of the equal dignity of states is a general principle of organization that applies in the American system and other federal systems. Under the American system, all states are equal in political authority. It is true that the powers of the federal government have expanded, as in interpretations of the commerce and welfare clauses, but the expansion has affected all states equally. No state has less dignity or less status than any other. In the American system, there is no high or low, no great or small state, despite differences in population, resources, or wealth. The same is true of the pan-American system (the OAS). Each member state has one vote, and the charter of the OAS guarantees each nation its territorial integrity and independence. All international differences are settled by peaceful procedures. An attack on one is an attack on all. No nation may use economic or political pressure to coerce another state. No one has a veto, and there are no privileged states in the system. All members have an equal place on the important OAS committees. Latin American nations are a neighbor of one of the greatest empires in history yet have no fear of imperialism.

In the Swiss Federation, the oldest federation in the world, members have identical legal status. The twenty-five Swiss cantons are of different sizes—from Zug with 92 square miles to Grissons with 2,773—and have widely different populations. Yet the federal government has limited powers, and the legislature is subject to the ballot initiative and referendum. For more than six hundred years, all disputes have been settled by arbitration. Since 1815, each canton has had one vote, and the federal government has surrendered the right of intervention. The federation has drawn strength from voluntary association in the establishment of its moral identity.[1]

The realists' answer to American exceptionalists, who in effect argued that the United States was not like other nations, derives from the study of history, and history teaches that Americans have not been immune from the constraints of interest and power. Faced with a succession of foreign-policy choices between intervention and neutrality in 1793, expansion and the status quo before the Mexican War and after the Spanish-American War, and choosing to oppose the Axis Powers in World War II against remaining aloof from the conflict, American leaders could not escape issues of interest and power.

Whatever their rhetoric, leaders have reached decisions not primarily from high moral principles but from judgments based on imperatives of national security and national self-preservation. On April 22, 1793, despite a treaty of friendship with France, President George Washington issued his neutrality proclamation. The secretary of the treasury, Alexander Hamilton, defended him in the famous *Pacificus* articles that appeared in the *Gazette of the United States*. A French critic of the neutrality proclamation, Citizen Genet, mobilized opposition to Washington, who was hung in effigy by an angry mob in the streets of Philadelphia. Hamilton asked, if the United States were to join France in a war against virtually all the rest of Europe, what risks would it run, what advantages could it expect, and what could it do to aid an ally? Realists maintain that these questions should always be raised regardless of formal or informal commitments.

1. Frank Tannenbaum, "The Balance of Power Versus the Coordinate State," *Political Science Quarterly*, XVII (June, 1952), 173, and "The American Tradition in Foreign Relations," *Foreign Affairs*, XXX (October, 1951), 31.

When decisions regarding war and peace are at issue, the United States must consider national interest.

As to the second example of foreign-policy choices, an answer was given by an American educator who was to become president. He explained, "Ease and prosperity have made us wish the whole world to be as happy and well to do as ourselves, and we have supposed that institutions and principles like our own were the simple prescription for making them so. And yet, when issues of our own interest arose, we have not been unselfish. We have shown ourselves kin to all the world, when it came to pushing an advantage." He went on to insist that our country's actions against Spain in the Floridas, against Mexico on the coasts of the Pacific, in our attitude toward the Spanish over control of the Mississippi River and later the French, and "the unpitying force with which we thrust the Indians to the wall whenever they stood in our way," were no different from those of other nations, whatever our claim that we were not as other nations. And in a statement that provides a matchless text in moral and political analysis, he observed:

> Even Mr. Jefferson, philanthropist and champion of peaceable and modest government though he was, exemplified this double temper of the people he ruled. "Peace is our passion," he had declared; but the passion abated when he saw the mouth of the Mississippi about to pass into the hands of France. Though he had loved France and hated England, he did not hesitate then what language to hold. "There is on the globe," he wrote to Mr. Livingston [U.S. ambassador to France], "one single spot the possessor of which is our natural and habitual enemy. The day that France takes possession of New Orleans seals the union of two nations, who, in conjunction, can maintain exclusive possession of the sea. From that moment, we must marry ourselves to the British fleet and nation. Our interests must march forward, altruists though we are; other nations must see to it that they stand off, and do not seek to stay us." [2]

The author of this penetrating analysis was not Richelieu, Bismarck, or Clemenceau, although they would have endorsed it. Instead, it was a young professor of political economy and jurisprudence at Princeton University whom Tannenbaum mistakenly

2. Woodrow Wilson, "Democracy and Efficiency," *Atlantic Monthly,* LXXVII (March, 1901), 293–94.

identified with unqualified American exceptionalism. Whatever his subsequent career in politics and crusade for a new international organization may have required, Woodrow Wilson's sober scholarly analysis suggests an awareness of the realities of American foreign policy and international politics that cannot be denied. American statesmen, including Wilson and Jefferson, have sometimes appealed to the public in the language of American exceptionalism, but their rhetoric has to be measured by the time and the purpose it was meant to serve.

As for the criticism that realism is in conflict with the equality of the units that make up the coordinate state, Tannenbaum's vision bears little relationship to reality. Early in the race for the 1996 Republican nomination for president, Governor Wilson of California debated whether to enter his party's race for the presidency. Without questioning Governor Wilson's attractiveness as a relatively moderate Republican candidate, can anyone suppose that the size of his state, its control of more than fifty votes in the Republican convention, and California's importance as one of the early Republican primaries were not factors? Federalism is sometimes cited as evidence of the equality of states. But federalism is basically concerned with the distribution of powers between the federal government and the states within a constitutional system of checks and balances. Except for their equality in the number of senators, the states vary greatly in influence because of "wealth, power, size, population or culture." Eighty-five years ago, another Columbia University political and constitutional historian asked, "Are the states equal under the Constitution?" His answer was, "The theory of equal states falls to the ground."[3]

The notion of the equality of states within regional organizations is also subject to question. Can anyone doubt that the United States has exercised hegemony within the Western Hemisphere? Or that England was the center of power in the British Commonwealth? Churchill's view of international organization assumed that the core of any regional or worldwide institution would be one or more major powers. Britain and France were such powers in the League of

3. Tannenbaum, "The Balance of Power," 177; William Archibald Dunning, *Essays on the Civil War and Reconstruction and Related Topics* (New York, 1931), 351.

Nations, and the United States has played such a role in the United Nations.

To recognize the differences in influence and power between nations is a fact of international politics, however difficult for some to accept. Small powers clearly have a role to play and lessons to offer the international community. They are often laboratories for social reform and staunch defenders of peace among nations. The first three secretaries-general of the United Nations were Norwegian, Swedish, and Burmese. Frequently, small and medium-size powers take the lead within international organizations, particularly in social and economic programs. Yet when international disputes and conflicts arise and one or more imperialistic powers threaten the international order, a nation or a coalition of states must rally support and organize resources in order to confront power with power. Painful as the lesson may be, to deny the reality of power is to misunderstand international politics.

The Classical Versus the Scientific Approach

No one should be surprised that writings and interpretations in every field of study compete for attention and acceptance. It has always been so in the history of thought, and studies of international relations are no exception. Not only revision but often the refutation of historical, philosophical, and legal theories may be the norm. Freud's writings led on to Jung and a host of post-Freudian views. With Karl Marx it was much the same. Successors build on what their forerunners have constructed. They rarely if ever sketch in their views on a blank sheet.

The relationship between the classical and the scientific approaches is of another order. The choice is not between a single formative view and various revisions and modifications but rather between two alternative perspectives. The classical view has a two-thousand-year history of philosophers undertaking to see the world whole and making "an unusually stubborn attempt to think clearly." It has its roots in philosophy, history, law, and the reflections of men of affairs. At the end of a long discourse on power and ideals, it calls on man's preeminent intellectual virtue—wisdom. Judgment is the cardinal virtue in politics, ranking above wisdom insofar as political choice is concerned. Judgment is the process in which practical morality comes into play. Judgment is coming to closure after weighing the alternatives, each with a heavy baggage of favorable and unfavorable elements. Judgment is choosing under fire with the hounds of time snapping at one's heels. Judgment in politics is what distinguishes a handful of leaders whom we celebrate for their political wisdom, among them Lincoln, Bismarck, Washington, Roosevelt, and Churchill. Judgment is a matter of hard and often excruciatingly painful choices. It is trial and error rather than infallibility or perfect vision.

Those who understand judgment have less to say about prediction than do the scientists of politics because the world with which judgment contends is a world of accidents and contingencies. To be specific, it is a world of the unpredictable. Judgment makes the best of imperfect information and human limitations. Judgment is action by imperfect humanity moving across a darkened stage without benefit of a script describing what has been, is now, or is yet to be. Judgment is sometimes the result of blind, painful groping. Judgment in politics is having the right political instincts.

Those who study politics are subject to many of the same limitations as those who practice politics. In a sense, the students and theorists of politics are themselves part of the problem. They stand inside, not outside, history. They bring to their study the same prejudices and predilections that men of affairs bring to the practice of politics. For the scientist in his laboratory, his attitude toward, say, cancer is basically irrelevant. The emotions he feels toward a particular gene are less important than his skills and training and his commitment to science. He works toward an ultimate scientific result, not toward a resolution of a policy problem by an early deadline with the public ready to confront him as critics. If a scientist's personal attitude toward a cancer gene is not likely to be determining, the same cannot be said about the attitude of the social and political observer or the economist. Marxists speak of Marxist scientific economics, yet even the most scientific Marxist economists predicate their science on the attainment or preservation of a Marxist economy. Keynesians, however rigorous their economics, presuppose the intervention of government into the economy, at least at crucial times and in key economic sectors, whereas noninterventionists presuppose that a healthy economy requires that the government stand aside.

Monetary economics is touted as a science, but its scientific objectivity is restricted to the precepts of monetarist economics. On fundamental issues such as human nature, international society, forms of government, and war and peace, international-relations scholars divide before, during, and after their research. Their findings in part reflect their underlying assumptions.

The champions of scientific research find support for their approach in the remarkable achievements of modern science. Who can imagine that anything but science could have carried mankind to the moon or made possible the docking of the spacecraft Apollo with the space station? What comparable successes can the classics offer? The wonders of genetic research would be impossible in the absence of science. In response to its critics, science justifies itself by pointing to breathtaking results. For the rest of mankind's problems, all that remains is to close the gap between the natural and social sciences, a gap for which cultural lag is responsible. Social scientists have been backward in the methods they employ, whereas natural science is forward looking. To become modern scientists, they must turn away from what some call intuitive guesses and base their analysis on mathematical proof and empirical verification. The answer to a true science is to be found not in "wisdom literature," as the late William Riker described the classical approach, but in the organization of testable proportions that will lead to truth. Science depends on material resources and concentrated man-hours. Or, as the late dean of a leading Midwest university once explained to the officer of a major foundation, a few million dollars will bring a theorist such as Morton Kaplan to the level of an Einstein.

Enthusiasm for a scientific approach to international relations has persisted for more than a half century. Its standing results less from its accomplishments than its ambitions, aspirations, and self-promotion. It has moved from an inquiry on the fringes of international relations to become a dominant approach. However the history of science in social science is written, self-promotion may prove to have been a short-term strength and a long-term disability. How different the debate between the scientific and the classical approach would have been if the claims for science had been more modest. Viewing science in greater modesty, most would agree that it has made important contributions to social and political understanding through election studies at the University of Michigan, Karl Hovland's research at Yale, Samuel Stouffer's research on the American soldier at Wisconsin, national-income studies, unemployment and underemployment research, and business-cycle theory. Some international-relations scholars would make similar claims for other theories, including social communication, bargaining theories, and peace research. With the exception of bargaining theory, however, consensus on success stories is limited. Furthermore, none of these advances, separately or together, come close to providing an overall theory of international behavior. Scientists like to make claims of breakthroughs in their respective fields. It may be significant that such claims are almost never sustained in international relations.

The fact is that the important questions in international relations are seldom addressed by scientific theories. Should the United States recognize Vietnam? What about U.S. intervention in Haiti? Should the Eastern European and Balkan countries be admitted to NATO? Ought the United States pay its dues to the United Nations? Should American troops serve under a foreign commander? Quantitative and behavioral theorists, more often than not, have little to say to such questions because on balance they require qualitative judgments. The subject matter comprises a virtually unmanageable number of variables. The unknowns are incommensurable. Factors to be assessed are in continuous flux. New elements inject themselves, most often without warning. Not only the data but the categories employed also lack fixed content and character. Social scientists, more than mature natural scientists, have a fetish for measurement, often addressed to immeasurable phenomena. Examples are national character and national resolve. The fate of nations in war and peace often hinges on the ability to confront harsh challenges and persevere. How are we to know in advance of a nuclear strike whether any particular nation has the will to survive?

It is fair, then, to ask where this leaves the debate. One tentative if not wholly satisfying answer is at the point at which the debate began. The student no less than the practitioner of international relations must navigate a stream in which the currents of continuity and change come together. History offers a road map of international relations with guideposts and warning signs along the way. Principles of foreign policy provide rough guidelines, not a map that gives directions for each twist and turn along the way. "Never fight a war on two major fronts if it can be avoided" is a precept to consider, but sound judgment is required in its application. "Treaties ought to be observed," but not if they weaken a nation's security. A small power ought not to ally itself with a great power, but it may be required to do so to restore a balance of power in a region. The fathers of international thought have amassed a storehouse of wisdom on the most perplexing problems. The deficiency of the scientific approach is that it rarely has much to say on issues that count most in war and peace.

Interdependence Versus the Nation-State

A third great debate came to the fore in the late 1970s with an emphasis on international interdependence. A forerunner of the debate was Wendell Wilkie, who was the Republican candidate for president in 1940. In his book *One World,* he argued that Americans were living in an interdependent world in which people were bound together by common economic interests. Later, David Mitrany was to suggest in his writings on functionalism that nationals of different countries who join together to ameliorate common economic and social needs may, through working together on an urgent problem, erode national sovereignty. He saw economic cooperation organized internationally on the model of the Tennessee Valley Authority spilling across national boundaries and building larger political communities. Mitrany was also cautious, however, about the size and extent of the geographic area in which functional cooperation could take place, even expressing doubts that it would spread across the European community, to say nothing of around the globe. Concurrent with the rise of functionalism, transnational cooperation was fostered by such new institutions as the International Court of Justice, the United Nations, and the network of Bretton Woods financial institutions established after World War II.

On the scholarly side, Robert O. Keohane and Joseph S. Nye are coauthors of a significant book on the international system.[4] They explain that the purpose of the book is to locate classical realist anal-

4. Robert O. Keohane and Joseph S. Nye, *Power and Interdependence: World Politics in Transition* (Boston, 1997).

ysis within a wider context of change and stability in the new era of interdependence. According to the authors, the world of the 1970s was a world without borders, a global village and an interdependent order in economics, communications, and human aspirations. They stress that their intent is not to replace realism with interdependence but to establish points of interconnection. The coauthors distinguish their views from those of the people they call traditionalists (the classical realists) and moderns, who believe that technology and social and economic transactions are changing the world and rendering nation-states obsolete. They proclaim that their goal is to distill and blend the wisdom derived from realism by constructing a theoretical framework for the political analysis of interdependence. Political realism, they suggest, proceeds from a model that stresses potential military conflict. Realists are slow to recognize new issues that do not center on military power. They argue that new international regimes are establishing new procedures, rules, and institutions to regulate and control transnational and interstate relations. National-security concerns were a product of the Cold War and were used by internationalists to generate support for increased American involvement in world affairs. With the end of the Cold War and the lessening of military concerns, interdependence began to have greater credibility than national security and greater explanatory power. Interdependence and economic concerns would become the hallmark of international relations in the post–Cold War era.

The theoretical contribution of interdependence thinking is grounded exclusively in recent history and in logical analysis rather than in-depth analysis of concrete historical examples from international politics. We are told that dependence means being influenced and coerced by external factors. At one point interdependence is described as the constituting of objective situations with reciprocal effects among countries or among different actors in different countries. The reputed effects result from international transactions—flows of money, goods, and people, and cultural and other exchanges—presumably without reference to their effects on international politics or the distribution of power in the world. What the authors consider most important is that the human interactions occurring across national boundaries have been doubling every ten years. After acknowledging that interdependence involves costs as well as benefits, inherent in the fact that independence carries the advantages of autonomy, the authors distinguish between a realist calculus and an interdependent one. According to realism, when one side in a balance of power situation succeeds in upsetting the status quo, its gain is the other side's loss—a zero-sum relation. If, however, most or all of the parties desire a stable status quo, they gain through cooperation. Although there are similarities, marked differences exist "between the traditional politics of military security and the politics of economic and ecological interdependence."[5] For the first time in international history, therefore, interdependency has found an autonomous method for guiding nations around political disputes that in the past often brought on military conflict.

Keohane and Nye also discuss the relationship between power and interdependence and provide a set of analytical concepts. They define *power* as control over resources or the potential to affect outcomes. The concept of *sensitivity* measures degrees of responsiveness in one country to changes in another. Japan, being heavily dependent on imported oil, was more *sensitive* in the early 1970s to increased oil prices than the United States. *Vulnerability* is measured by the effectiveness or lack thereof of a country's efforts to create raw materials that are lacking or in short supply, and at what cost. The authors also discuss symmetrical and asymmetrical interdependence. *International regimes* are intermediate factors between the power structure of an international system and the political and international bargaining that takes place in the system. Regime changes take place more rapidly in some areas than in others, for example, in international monetary policy, as compared with the world's oceans.

Finally, the coauthors compare realism with complex interdependence. In the latter, multiple channels between nations exist, including interstate, transgovernmental, and transnational relations. The agenda of interstate relations has no clear hierarchy of issues. Military force is not used by governments toward other governments within a region when complex interdependence prevails. Apparently, to the extent that policies were based on this prediction, the breakup of the former Yugoslavia caught the two theorists by surprise.

5. *Ibid.,* 10.

Nye and Keohane have made a marginal contribution to the central issues in the study of international politics. The post–Cold War world they envisage is more evident in theory than practice. Realists have never doubted that international cooperation in social and economic spheres was more likely than in contested political spheres. The U.N. specialized agencies illustrate the progress that is possible in nonpolitical arenas. Yet even the specialized agencies and the United Nations are the children of nation-states on which they depend for financing and popular support. Because Nye and Keohane in their writings reflect the spirit of the times and their euphoria at the prospect of an interdependent world is as great as that surrounding the birth of the United Nations in 1945, they failed to anticipate the rising tide of nationalism and hostility to the United Nations and a new form of isolationism that threatens aspects of interdependence. One reason is certainly the ahistorical approach of interdependence theory. Nye and Keohane make reference to very few historical examples from before 1945. The other reason is their zeal to distinguish their views from those of others, leading them to misrepresent and distort the realist viewpoint. Even a hasty reading of *Politics Among Nations* would have revealed not a hierarchical preference for military conflict but rather a desire for its prevention. Simply reading the book's subtitle (*The Struggle for Power and Peace*) could have saved them from their mistaken view of realism.

Another conspicuous failing of *Power and Interdependence* is its false reading of some of the changes occurring in international relations. In part, such failures result from theorists straining for parsimonious and overly simple theoretical definitions. We are told that interdependence means being influenced by external factors. What nation is not influenced in this way, including the world's one remaining superpower? International transactions of all kinds are said to create effects on international politics. Is there no difference between the meetings of the NATO defense chiefs over Bosnia and, say, tourists enjoying themselves on holiday or an international conference of stamp collectors? Are national and unit differences, which have existed since time immemorial, no longer relevant simply because human interdependence is doubling every ten years? Are the authors correct in assuming that most or all of the parties engaged in the politics of economic and ecological interdependence will desire a stable status quo within their area of cooperation? What about Yugoslavia? Was this true between the United States and most of the Third World countries at the Brazil environmental summit? In other words, did concern with ecological interdependence eliminate the sharp differences between North-South and industrial–Third World countries? Will the contacts between nonstate entities such as multinational corporations erase national conflicts and differences? Or do multilateral efforts sometimes provoke nationalistic reactions?

Keohane and Nye have identified an important sector of international relations, but in their zeal to distinguish their views from others they have fallen victim to a disease that plagues most revisionists. That is eclecticism, which, in the name of blending and distilling all wisdom, bends and distorts the views it seeks to criticize to fit its own theoretical purposes. Further, eclecticism is so often banal because it drains from the theories it claims to analyze what is essential and of enduring value. Also, Nye and Keohane offer in effect a prophecy about the state of the world after the Cold War, a prophecy assumed to point up what other approaches have failed to recognize. Instead, international and domestic politics are moving in precisely the opposite direction from the Keohane and Nye prophecy, with declining support for the United Nations measured (and the authors have a penchant for measurement) by the state of bankruptcy into which the organization has fallen. Furthermore, their discussion of power and interdependence is marked by an array of clever formulas and definitions appropriately charted and quantified but with none of the philosophical profundity we associate with major theorists from Thucydides to Morgenthau. Finally, this work was undoubtedly begun at the height of cultural exchange in the 1960s and 1970s. It illustrates the perils of identifying too closely with the spirit of the times. Interdependence and international cooperation were then in vogue, in contrast with the controversy over U.S. actions in Vietnam and Nicaragua. Today, efforts to bring multilateralism to bear on conflicts in Africa, North Korea, and for a time in the former Yugoslavia—even efforts by NATO—have had little positive effect. These criticisms leave open the question of whether a new and more realistic approach may yet salvage the political importance of such bodies as NATO. They do throw a shadow over the panaceas that are offered by renegades like Nye and Keohane.

Systematic Thinking Versus Systems Theory

For half a century, the evolution of international relations has advanced toward more systematic thinking. Much as the study of American government had its origins in civics, the beginnings of international studies sought to increase knowledge of current events. The objective of the former was good government; of the latter, a better-informed citizenry. The bible for those seeking to expand their view of the world was the New York *Times*. Not far behind were other national newspapers, including the Louisville *Courier-Journal* and the St. Louis *Post-Dispatch*. To generalize, access to responsible reporting of all the current events fit to print was seen as an end in itself.

Although the enhancement of public-affairs information is a worthy goal, it falls short of preparing one to think more clearly about world affairs. At best, information can increase the amount of useful data without pointing the way to understanding. The question is always, knowledge for what? Woodrow Wilson's most important contribution, however ill fated in the end, may have been in prophesying the birth of a new world order that promised peace and unity. For a quarter of a century, Wilsonianism influenced American thinking about international relations. The idea of an international community and a league to enforce peace had roots both in history and in utopianism. Wilson looked back and looked ahead—back to the history of more limited international experiments, such as the Concert of Europe (Wilson in fact spoke and wrote of a concert for peace) and the international arbitration movement, and ahead to the League of Nations. Whereas the current-events approach had led to a vast proliferation of information and data, Wilson and those who followed him gathered that information around a set of goals that included the League, national self-determination, and world community. Wilsonianism presented international studies with a framework that gave thinking about international affairs a purpose and direction.

The problem with a reformist approach, however, is that the children of reform all too often grow disillusioned and trade idealism for cynicism, grand visions for a sense of guilt, and resolve for resignation. For example, Marxism has multiple flaws and assumptions, but anti-Marxists are wrong in arguing it is devoid of all idealism.

They overlook Marx's overriding concern with the alienated individual. According to Marx, the worker under capitalism is enslaved and dehumanized by capitalism. When property is done away with, however, greed and envy will disappear and the essence of humanity will be restored through life in an egalitarian society. Yet whatever idealism may have been present at the birth of Marxism, cynicism soon took its place. Marxism's false idealism was destroyed by a hard utopianism that justified every act of cruelty and barbarism by invoking the Communist utopia. Further, promotion of the League of Nations was a requirement for professors, written into every endowed chair for the teaching of international relations in the leading American universities. By the 1930s, support for a future international organization was driven as much by a sense of guilt for the rejection of the League by the U.S. Senate as by confidence that the League would assure peace. Americans had rejected the building that their president had wrought. Finally, the people had grown weary, as after each great war, and sought rest from their labors. Their wartime resolve was weakened. They became resigned to conflicts around the world. In the end, they were reawakened less by Hitler than by Pearl Harbor.

Nonetheless, Wilsonianism drew strength from the nobility of its vision more than from the realities with which it successfully grappled. It was grounded less in systematic thinking than in the passions it inspired. When President Wilson, arriving in Paris for the Versailles peace conference, was hailed as the messiah by throngs of French people, his appeal derived less from systematic thinking than from the dream of a world united and at peace. To discover Wilson's more rigorous thinking, we must return to his days as a young professor and educator, when he was engaged in the search for truth, not rallying the masses to a towering moral purpose. Because his mission was not the same, the means that he chose and his intellectual and political strategy were different in the two stages of his life.

After World War II, students of international relations set forth on a path toward more systematic thinking. The rhetoric of some leaders, at least some of the time, was reminiscent of Wilsonianism. Cordell Hull, secretary of state in the Roosevelt administration, announced that the creation of the United Nations ensured the end of power politics, alliances, spheres of influence, and the balance of power. President Franklin D. Roosevelt spoke in a similar vein on a few occasions, but his political instincts led him, usually unerringly, toward a more realistic if not a systematic approach. He was a political genius, especially in national affairs, who had internalized somehow the best fruits of the more systematic thought of others. To adapt another phrase, much as the uneducated speak prose without knowing it, he acted according to realist precepts without having studied its intellectual history, except for naval history.

In the postwar period, new schools of thought began to appear in the universities and colleges and in the front ranks of diplomacy and journalism. In Book 5 of the *Republic,* Plato argues that knowledge without "forms" is impossible. He contrasts the forms for the knowledge of craftsmen in making beds and tables with the knowledge philosophers require to maintain good intra- and intercity relations. Dialectic inquiry leads the philosopher in the direction of truth, doing away with hypothesizing and the testing of assumptions, and proceeding to first principles. In a rough and approximate sense, Plato's idea of "forms" corresponds to the idea of systematic thought. Much as Plato made use of forms and types and established a hierarchy of forms with philosophy and politics at the top, postwar thinkers have sought an ordering framework for understanding international relations by placing international politics at the top of a hierarchy of actions. Plato illustrated the point by explaining that as the flute player guides the flute maker to make flutes that are "fine and right," the "philosopher-king" directs the flute player to know what kind of music is fine or right in the state.

In international-relations thinking, the existence of a hierarchy culminating in the primacy of the nation-state bears some relationship to Plato's idea of forms. The development of more systematic thinking on national government in the 1930s was characterized by greater emphasis on the forces of politics, including political parties and pressure groups. Earlier, the emphasis had fallen heavily on the study of the Constitution. For example, until early in the twentieth century the role of the president was one of expounding and teaching the Constitution. Later, the president used his "bully pulpit" to introduce legislation and justify policy. The difference between Wilson's role in proclaiming goals and values, and that of later presidents well described as sheepdogs seeking to round up supporters for policies, shows the evolving role of the presidency. In the nineteenth century, presidents saw their job as explaining and "speaking" the Constitution and in the twentieth century as defending policies.

Political realism, while going as far back as the Founding Fathers if not Thucydides, has sought to provide "forms" for the post–World War II era that are intended to convey the essence of international politics. Realism begins with things as they are and considers change in relation to circumstances and, in particular, the obstacles to change. It offers a framework or "form" within which the factors of "interest" and "power" can be understood. Realism undertakes to be systematic in studying power politics, the rivalries among states, the balance of power, international institutions, war and peace, national interest, diplomacy, and types of foreign policy. It seeks the ordering of data that would otherwise remain disparate and incomprehensible.

Realism aims to understand international politics within history. Its method is inductive; its focus is on the unique and the recurrent in history. Some events occur only once, but because there are patterns to history, others are members of a class of events. In reflecting on the unique and the general, Montaigne observed that if all humans were different, we could not distinguish man from beast. If they were all the same, we could not distinguish one person from another. Historical events have similar characteristics; some are unique and must be treated as such. Others are recurrent and help us understand theoretical propositions about politics.

Realists also question the view that science is the monopoly of certain behavioral or quantitative thinkers. Reinhold Niebuhr argued that history was an empirical science, exacting in the collection and classifying of information. The good historian is as rigorous in testing information and sources as the scientist in his laboratory. To survive, a theory has to meet the test of logical consistency and empirical validation. It has to find confirmation through meeting the standards of logical analysis and of historical experience. Does history bear it out?

Realism as a more systematic approach than Wilsonian idealism has taken many forms. The writings of theorists such as Morgenthau were efforts to create a general theory of politics and international politics. Others sought to provide theories having to do with some segment of international experience: deterrence theory, balance of power theory, bargaining theory, the theory of diplomacy, and development theories. Some proceeded on the basis of historical analysis, for example, Alfred Vagts on balance of power theory. Others introduced novel quantitative and analytical techniques, as with Thomas Schelling's bargaining theory. The intellectual foundations of many such theories, whether consciously in the mind of the theorist or not, went back to realism. Each of these theories made a contribution, whether large or small, to the development of more systematic thinking.

The break from post–World War II approaches that are described as traditional realism came with systems theory and neorealism. The writings of University of California political scientist Kenneth Waltz provide the most important example of an emerging school of thought. Waltz's early work was *Man, the State and War: A Theoretical Analysis,* published first in 1954 and again in 1959. It was a study in response to encouragement from an often-overlooked theorist who devoted much of his scholarly life to guiding and directing the work of others—William T. R. Fox, the director of the War and Peace Institute of Columbia University. Fox was Waltz's mentor. In the foreword to the book, Fox observed that it was incumbent on the scholar to draw on existing storehouses of knowledge, and such a storehouse "least systematically inventoried for its usefulness for international relations is classical western political thought."[6] In political theory, Waltz's mentors were Herbert Deane and Franz Neumann. None of the questions Western thinkers addressed were more central to Waltz's concerns than the causes of war and conditions of peace. The format of his book was designed to examine the answers of various theorists to questions of war and peace and, in alternate chapters, to examine their implications for controversies regarding ideologies and problems, such as international socialism and the coming of the First World War. Waltz at the outset made clear that he was more interested in increasing the chances of peace and decreasing the incidence of war. To ask about the elimination or outlawing of war was the wrong question. He was not always consistent on these points.

Waltz's most memorable contribution in *Man, the State and*

6. William T. R. Fox, Foreword to Kenneth N. Waltz, *Man, the State and War: A Theoretical Analysis* (1954; rpr. New York, 1959), i.

War was a systematic approach to the major causes of war. Calling upon a fairly traditional mode of analysis but with intimations of his later study, he developed a threefold typology of causes of war, locating the primary causes within man, within the state, and within the international system of states. Later, he referred to them as the three images or three levels of analysis of international relations. According to the first image, wars arise because of human nature and mankind's behavior, whether through selfishness, misdirected aggression, impulses, or stupidity. Man's nature appears to be primary; all others are secondary causes. As Waltz sees it, the elimination of war therefore depends on mankind's enlightenment and improvement. Education is Waltz's remedy for war at this point in his thinking.

Curiously, he had little to say about limiting war by restraining human nature through systems of checks and balances and political or legal rules and constraints. Working with human nature as it is to create conditions of political equilibrium and to strengthen international order received less emphasis than doing away with war through education. Does this suggest a contradiction or at least a certain tension with his earlier statement about the incidence of war and peace and the later stages in his thinking? Moreover, having said that man's nature is a primary cause of war, he later asserts that human nature is not determinative because it is an ambiguous factor at work everywhere in "Sunday schools and brothels, philanthropic organizations and gangs."[7] To this, Waltz's critics ask, does its application everywhere rule out its influence more specifically on war?

What set Waltz apart in *Man, the State and War* was his associating concepts of theory, such as the three images, with the contributions of major political theorists, especially Spinoza, Kant, and Rousseau. Of the three, he returns again and again to Rousseau. In this he is the child of his political-theory mentor, Franz Neumann. He followed the explication of each of the three images with related case studies. In this he was responsive to Fox. The studies included a review of behavioral science weighed against an analysis of the insights of political theorists on man and human behavior. He then discussed the internal structure of states as seen through the eyes of

7. *Ibid.*, 80–81.

political theorists. He juxtaposed this image with an essay on international socialism and World War I. Finally, he turned to the image that, even then, appeared most important to him—the international system, conflict, and international anarchy, illustrated by a case study entitled "Economics, Politics, and History."

No one who reads the six essays (and, as he states in the preface, I was one of three friends and reviewers who read the original manuscript in its entirety) can be other than impressed, even if sometimes critical. In introducing the subject of human nature, Waltz lists political theorists who attribute the existence of evil actions to evil in human nature. For Waltz, our miseries are ineluctably the product of our nature. The root of all evil is man, and thus he is himself the root of the specific evil—war. He quotes John Milton: "The perverseness of our folly is so bent, that we should never cease hammering out of our own hearts, as it were out of a flint the seeds and sparkles of new misery to ourselves, we all were in a blaze again." For many thinkers, this perspective on human nature is an article of faith, and Waltz calls the roll of philosophers such as Augustine, Luther, Malthus, Jonathan Swift, and Reinhold Niebuhr as well as philosophers and statesmen such as Spinoza and Bismarck. If this view of man as the source of human conflict is sound, then the early peace plans of the French monk Cruce and the statesman Sully are idle dreams. So are attempts to explain recurrent wars in economic terms.[8]

As I read Waltz's manuscript, I concluded that he sometimes misinterprets the writers he mentions—at least those I know best—because they in fact saw man as both good *and* evil, intermingling the most humane and generous motives with profoundly powerful emotions rooted in self-centeredness and self-interest. Waltz was less interested in this issue, however, than in addressing with Rousseau the influence of society on man. Does man make society or does society make man? This question persists down to the present, not only in international relations but also in controversies over most social programs. Rousseau and Plato believe that a bad polity makes man bad and a good polity makes man good. Waltz agrees to the extent that we need to understand both man and society in order to

8. *Ibid.*, 3–5.

comprehend human behavior and war. It would be difficult to show that Niebuhr, Morgenthau, or Lippmann ignored the state and international society.

The gravamen of Waltz's argument is that the theorist who studies the causes of war must do so from not one level of analysis but from all three. I see little difference, except in emphasis, between his view and that of the traditional realists. The intellectual routes they follow in reaching their conclusions are obviously different, however. Where they differ is in assigning permanent characteristics to human nature, which for traditional realists are enduring and for Waltz are apparently subject to change. He emphasizes that men who seek to behave decently need some assurance that others will not take advantage of their decency. States in the state system need similar reassurance. What he ignores is that this is true a fortiori in the family, in personal relations, and in every dimension of the human drama, a point that realists such as Niebuhr present in a far more profound account of man and society.

Although the three images in Waltz's *Man, the State and War* are valuable concepts in ordering information and indeed have proven the most durable aspect of his theory, the book has another notable strong point. Whatever one's conclusion on the merits of Waltz's approach to theory, he offers, sometimes in passing, a host of perceptive impressions and reflections that enhance understanding. He draws on a vast literature from history, philosophy, and politics. He evaluates themes such as optimism and pessimism, the simultaneously finite and infinite nature of man, reason and passion, and ultimate and proximate justice. Despite his later conversion to the philosophy of science, Waltz's case study of the behavioral sciences in *Man, the State and War* is relentless in exposing illusions and a troublesome vagueness. He relates, for example, the proposal at the height of the Cold War by psychiatrist James Miller to plant in the Soviet Union one thousand trained social scientists disguised as Russians, to sample public opinion in order to learn what Russians were thinking. Gordon Allport proposed that buildings be arranged so that delegates to international organizations such as the United Nations would pass through the playground of a nursery school. The recommendations of behavioral scientists, Waltz observes, are "either hopelessly vague or downright impossible to follow."[9] The advice given by one contradicts that of another. Much of their vagueness results, Waltz explains, from their unwillingness or inability to proceed in their research within a political framework. Ironically, behavioral scientists were the first to make the case for science among postwar social scientists, yet they are targeted. Waltz's turn to this subject must be seen as the third or fourth wave of interest in science among social scientists, as such attention has waxed and waned.

In his discussion of the second image, Waltz once again makes clear why he considers the state and the state system central to understanding the causes of war. He maintains that everything is related to the first image or human nature. Although some writers would argue that this makes focusing on man's nature fundamental, Waltz concludes otherwise. Whereas the duality of human nature helps explain why men can both make war and negotiate peace, Waltz sees this as evidence that human nature is not ambiguous but insufficient to make it a primary causal factor. He argues that events relating to war are so varied and numerous that human nature is too amorphous to be the primary determinant. Realists like Morgenthau and Niebuhr explain that when a nation-state plagued by internal strife turns to war, it is simply evidence of how a weak regime seeks to regain authority and power. By contrast, Waltz sees it as substantiating his thesis that the internal structure of states—more than human nature—is a determining cause of war. He is unwilling, however, to accept without qualification the opposite conclusion that stable and democratic states are everywhere the guardians of peace. The reason may be that he is too familiar with the fate of earlier claims, such as Marx's promise that eliminating private property, Kant's claim that the multiplication of democracies and republican regimes, or Woodrow Wilson's prediction that national self-determination would ensure peace and tranquility.

In connection with his discussion of the internal structure of states, Waltz asks how states change their structure. This leads him to discuss intervention as a possible mechanism of change. Here the liberal political theorists he discusses fall into two categories: optimistic noninterventionists, who include Kant, Cobden, and Bright,

9. *Ibid.*, 65.

and messianic interventionists—Paine, Mazzini, and Woodrow Wilson. The latter group set out to make the world democratic; the former in their optimism about the world would use force only to safeguard their own democracies. Among recent exponents of the latter view was Walter Hines Page, ambassador to England during the First World War, who asserted, "You cannot conceive of a democracy that will set out on a career of conquest." To this the late Dean Inge replied, "Ask a Mexican, a Spaniard, a Filipino, or a Japanese."[10] When Tito broke with Stalin and shattered the myth of monolithic communism, Roy Macrides explained that "two national Communist countries were bound to show the same incompatibilities that bourgeois national countries have shown in the past." Whatever the internal structure of states, the international political environment often determines how national states behave, leading Waltz to emphasize the third image as a primary cause of war.

The third image, then, brings Waltz to the most fundamental and final determinant of war—what he considers the most inclusive nexus. The first and second images for him acquire meaning in the light of the third. International anarchy is at the top of the hierarchy of images. Each state pursues its own interests and employs force when necessary to its ends. At this point, Waltz returns to his three political theorists. Spinoza is a first-image theorist who explains war and violence as the result of human imperfections or quarrels among those for whom passion replaces reason. For Kant, men live both in the world of sense and experience (*phenomena*) and in the world of understanding (*noumena*), which cannot be experienced. If men lived wholly in the latter, they would act in accordance with the categorical imperative. They would follow Kant's injunction to so act that they could wish their action to be a universal law or guide for all mankind. But the world of phenomena, of sense, impulse, and inclination, overcomes reason. Within the state, an adequate political system makes possible ethical behavior. No such system is attainable internationally, however, and Kant therefore acknowledges that perpetual peace is not inevitable but merely "not unthinkable."

Once more, it is to Rousseau that Waltz turns. Kant had proposed a voluntary federation of states. Rousseau would substitute as

10. William R. Inge, *Lay Thoughts of a Dean* (New York, 1926), 116–17.

the remedy for war a form of federal government for states that places every state voluntarily under the authority of the law. Yet how can it enforce the law without waging war against defectors? Rousseau responds that the states of Europe are in a condition of balance wherein one state cannot dominate all the rest. Thus a necessary margin of force will always be available to the federation to hold members in check.

The international system ultimately is the determinant of war and peace. It offers a social structure that provides institutional restraints and methods for adjusting and bringing interests into balance. In *Man, the State and War,* Waltz argues that there are only two solutions to the problem of international anarchy. One is to impose effective controls on independent and imperfect states. The other is to free states from living in the realm of the contingent, the accidental, and the imperfect by making states good, so that they are no longer particular wills but approach the universal will. Kant sought the answer through a compromise: through the universalism of republicanism, states would become good enough so they would accept and obey voluntarily. Rousseau rejects Kant's compromise, saying even Kant's somewhat good states are particular, as illustrated by the example of the stag hunt. Five men, all suffering from hunger, join in a stag hunt satisfied they can overcome their hunger by sharing one-fifth of the animal they trap. When a hare comes into view, one of them pursues and captures the hare, and in the process the stag escapes. The defector, chasing the hare is motivated by hunger but also by fear that another might leave his post and seize the hare, leaving all the rest as hungry as before.

What is the way out? For most political theorists it is for individual states to escape from the state of nature to that of the civil state. For Rousseau, the state may become an organic unit in a deeper sense than Spinoza understood. Under certain conditions it may actualize the general will to do what is best for its members considered collectively. Public spirit or patriotism is the necessary basis for the good state, and Rousseau feared it may have been waning in Europe. However, patriotism fused with nationalism becomes an all-powerful force involving the integration of the masses into a common political form. This idea runs through Rousseau's political writings, but he doubts it is possible beyond a circumscribed area such as the city-state. If all nations were content to sustain their own national unity and public spirit, peace might be possible, but as Rousseau writes: "However salutary it may be in theory to obey the dictates of public spirit, it is certain that politically and even morally, those dictates are likely to prove fatal to the man who persists in observing them with all the world when no one thinks of observing them towards him."[11]

In concluding, Waltz returns to his preoccupation with the third image of the state system. Ostensibly, he agrees with Alexander Hamilton and John Jay, who succeed where Waltz is only partly successful in relating first-image considerations to third-image propositions. It was Hamilton in *Federalist* 5 who warned that to assume a lack of hostile motives among states is to forget that men are "ambitious, vindictive and rapacious." He also wrote of the vanity of kings, the folly of assemblies, and the dominance of commercial interests. All these tendencies in individuals and groups connect human nature with conflicts in international society. By contrast, Waltz in his final comments points to third-image analysis as the means for avoiding "the tendency of some realists to attribute the necessary amorality or even immorality, of world politics to the inherently bad character of man." For Waltz, it remains true that "a foreign policy based on this image of international relations is neither moral nor immoral, but embodies merely a reasoned response to the world about us.[12] Although first and second images describe the forces in world politics and the determinants of policy, Waltz leaves to third-image thinking the resolution and accommodation of conflicting interests. Significantly, he makes only one brief reference to diplomacy, citing Metternich and Bismarck, whose places, he explains, are being taken by national politicians. He quotes Hans Kelsen on interests and justice: "Justice is an irrational ideal. However indispensable it may be for the volition and action of men, it is not subject to cognition. Regarded from the point of view of rational cognition, there are only interests, and hence conflicts of interest." Waltz translates this statement into terms of action by an effective decision-making authority or third-image analysis.

When one comes to the end of this immensely challenging book,

11. Jean-Jacques Rousseau, *A Lasting Peace Through the Federation of Europe and the State of War,* trans. C. E. Vaughan (London, 1917), 238.
12. *Ibid.*

one is struck by a paradox. What is most original and satisfying about it is also its major weakness. The author is so determined to sustain his three levels of analysis that they become not a source of illumination but a straitjacket. Waltz's overarching goal is to construct a coherent deductive theory founded on the structure of the international-security environment. In *Man, the State and War,* he wrote systematically about his subject. In *Theory of International Politics,* he undertook to develop a systemic theory. In the former, he gives content to the three levels of analysis by calling on philosophers and making them fit his causal hierarchy. In the latter, he gives short shrift to first- and second-image examples and ideas. In other writings he complains that "adding the internal to the external dimension of foreign policy makes for many complications."[13]

In contrast with Niebuhr and other realist theorists, he uses examples of first-image theorists whose discussion of human nature, he suggests, has little direct relevance for the state or international society. Has he read Niebuhr, who called on those who would understand international morality to search out international standards that reflect the norms of the whole without destroying the integrity of the parts? It is one thing to point to hand-picked first-image optimists who "betray a naïveté in politics," leading to the conclusion that views on human nature have little to contribute to an understanding of the state or international society. It is something else to dismiss the greats of political theory and international politics, including Niebuhr and Augustine, as having little to say about second- and third-image questions. Moreover, not only Niebuhr but other political philosophers are also forced into molds that more often extinguish than express their deeper insights and theories.

Furthermore, a problem that is compounded in Waltz's later writings, and especially in *Theory of International Politics,* is his commitment to a deductive form of theory that makes no concessions to the lessons of history. Where history and philosophy are intertwined, as in the writings of Thucydides or essays on the balance of power by David Hume or Alfred Vagts, their separation takes away much of the context that Waltz intends to preserve when he defends the causal primacy of the international political environment. His theory

13. Kenneth N. Waltz, *Foreign Policy and Democratic Politics: The American and the British Experience* (Boston, 1967), v.

lacks historical ballast. In the same way that Nye and Keohane con-centrate almost exclusively on contemporary history, Waltz writes mainly about the world after World War II. Thus his theory is a Cold War product carved out of superpower relations in an era of bipolarity and is based on the assumption of the irreversibility of communism and the maintenance of an international system under the sway of the superpowers.

In some minds, this may justify a retreat from inductive theoriz-ing. Yet it also coincides with Waltz's flight from historical complexity to third-image parsimony, narrowing his field of vision, compressing historical inquiry, and turning back a fifty-year advance in systematic thinking and international theorizing. *Theory of International Politics* continues the main themes of *Man, the State and War.* It does so in the idiom of science. Waltz begins with the complaint that interna-tional theory is not cumulative, a complaint Fox has directed against all of social science. Yet Fox more than Waltz was still open to other schools of thought, whether or not they embraced Waltz's meth-odology. Waltz's pursuit of theory leads him to identify the inter-national system as the first cause and prime mover and to relegate first- and second-image analysis to ever more subordinate roles. He leaves little room for exploring human nature in depth or analyzing the nature of the state. Yet these are the areas in which international-relations literature is most rich. If he subordinated first- and second-image analysis in *Man, the State and War,* he virtually abandoned them in *Theory of International Politics.* In the former work, Waltz had two thousand years of political theory and political experience to draw on explicitly—and implicitly—for its bearing on interna-tional politics. In the latter, he supports his findings with intriguing if highly abstract studies and reflections on methodology derived from the philosophy of science. Some of the studies may be sugges-tive, but none is definitive for politics. Looking back to the 1950s, the parallel may be the invoking of Einstein and Freud on war instead of Clausewitz or Machiavelli. In comparison with some present-day scientists, the former at least paid heed to human nature.

In a discussion of neorealism and realism, the observer is finally brought face to face with three fundamental questions. First, what is the purpose or intention of the theorist? Second, what are the sources with which the theorist works? Third, to what extent does the particular theory meet both empirical and logical tests? Is the theory consistent with the facts that are most relevant to its purpose? Is it logically consistent within the framework it seeks to establish? Does it proceed with logical necessity from its assumptions and premises? Is it consistent within itself?

Arriving at an answer to the first question, if based on the assumption that human motivation for major creative endeavors such as *Theory of International Politics* or *Politics Among Nations* can be reduced to a single factor, is itself questionable. Can anyone identify with confidence a single cause for one's actions, whether today or last week or ten years ago? Literary theory and interpretative studies of drama which, in an earlier phase of the discipline, undertook to focus on human motivation, have shifted to social and institutional factors and the scrutiny of an unfolding story. It happens that I know what the neorealist Waltz and the realist Morgenthau saw as the purpose of their pioneering studies. In the early 1960s, Waltz and I were members of a fellowship committee whose task was to select for awards graduate students from around the country engaged in writing doctoral dissertations. Waltz's important first book was fresh in my mind, and I asked about his next project. He responded that he was not satisfied with the theoretical rigor of *Man, the State and War* and planned to devote several years exclusively to the study of the history and philosophy of science. His reaction was more restrained than I remember Morton Kaplan's being some years before when I asked if he intended to return at some time to the policy studies he conducted at the Brookings Institution. Kaplan had responded that he was ashamed of his earlier work for its lack of theoretical rigor. He wished he could destroy all the copies in circulation. Two extraordinarily able scholars came to look on the transforming role of science as the route to elevating the level of theory and scholarly research.

I have no doubt as to Morgenthau's intention. He had a threefold purpose in writing *Politics Among Nations*. He saw himself as developing a coherent theory that from a practical standpoint would serve the cause of peace—hence his subtitle *The Struggle for Power and Peace*. Further, he meant to throw into question the validity of a certain approach to international politics, especially with respect to human nature and the nature of politics. His earlier treatise, *Scientific*

Man, foreshadowed *Politics Among Nations.* In both works, he condemned the notion that the use of the scientific method in the study of politics and international politics would yield revolutionary new answers and transform policy and understanding. He especially challenged the idea that science would assure predictability.

As to the second fundamental question, Waltz explained in our luncheon conversation that the main sources of his study would come from the philosophy of science. Who can believe that he would have spent years immersing himself in the literature of science unless he were confident it offered answers to an understanding of international politics? Indeed, one looks in vain through the 250 pages of *Theory of International Politics* for serious reservations concerning the scientific approach. Thanks to Franz Neumann, however, who introduced Waltz to Rousseau, and William T. R. Fox, who never bargained away his lifelong interest in international history, Waltz's book draws on a few of the more traditional political theorists (by page eight he has finished with the three references he makes to Plato and Aristotle, and he has nothing to say about traditional normative theorists from Augustine to Niebuhr) to illustrate aspects of his theoretical structure. Nevertheless, he must be distinguished from theorists such as Kaplan, who are determined to avoid the slightest contamination of the purity of their theory through the introduction of a single concrete historical example.

Morgenthau's use of sources is quite different from Waltz's. Like Herbert Butterfield and Martin Wight of the British Committee on the Theory of International Relations, Morgenthau looked to history, political theory, philosophy, and law as the raw stuff of theory. He turned to history as past politics to be molded into a viable theory of international politics. It remained for a distinguished British historian and political realist to describe the sources of the realist approach. He wrote that the group took as its mandate an inquiry "into the nature of the international state system, the assumption and ideas of diplomacy, the principles of foreign policy, the ethics of international relations and war." Butterfield expressed greater concern "with the historical than the contemporary, with the normative than the scientific, with the philosophical than the methodological, with principles than with policy." Often overlooked is the extent to which the history of war or diplomacy provides a treasure trove of practical wisdom forever worthy of study. Underlying all the sources with which realism must grapple are moral and normative issues that scientists admit exist beyond the boundaries of science. For Butterfield, "The underlying aim . . . is to clarify the principles of prudence and moral obligation."[14] Not only are the sources the two theories employ largely different from each other, but they rest on underlying assumptions that are irreconcilable and in conflict. Yet much of neorealist theory denies the conflict and invites science to take over international-relations theory.

Third, Waltz and the neorealists question whether empiricism or facts have anything to do with scientific explanations of international politics. In *Theory of International Politics,* Waltz asserts that a theory may have some relation to the real world, but the two must forever remain separate and apart. "Reality will be congruent neither with a theory nor a model that may represent it."[15] For thinkers such as Karl Popper, to whom theory is no more than "conjectural knowledge," history and experience exert no restraint on theorizing. Without qualification, neorealism chooses the deductive over the inductive approach. The task of the theorist, as Waltz's drawing on Kuhn makes clear, is to set forth a novel or original paradigm that is capable of generating new understanding. Kuhn's vision of science takes the place of the old vision built on the testing of researchable hypotheses to be dealt with experimentally and, in the end, falsified or confirmed. For realists, in contrast to neorealists, the constraints of reality and history place limits on paradigmatic thinking. Rigor and relevance are seen in relationship to each other. Neither can be absolute.

Niebuhr tells of participating in a meeting at the height of the Cold War as a consultant to George F. Kennan's policy planning staff. Kennan opened the discussion by asking those seated around the table to assume that with respect to the arms-control issue, the Soviet Union and Russia did not exist. Niebuhr found such an exercise highly irrelevant and questioned its utility. History and experience, which provide the context not only for realism but also for the behavioral social sciences, are considered by the neorealists a realm separate and apart from theory. They eliminate the creative tension sepa-

14. Butterfield and Wight, eds., *Diplomatic Investigations,* 11, 12, 13.

15. Kenneth N. Waltz, *Theory of International Politics* (Reading, Mass., 1979), 6–7.

rating the two. Nor do Waltz or most neorealists strictly adhere to their own canon, for when they speak of patterns and structures that sustain the status quo, they inevitably have in mind historical examples. It would be going too far to charge that neorealism is ahistorical, yet at the very least it is hopelessly ambivalent about history. On the one hand, it embraces the deeply ingrained ideology of the scientific profession that science and history are distinct. On the other hand, Waltz's text, especially from Chapter 6 to the conclusion, is replete with historical examples. Science questions the relevance of history for theory, yet it places the highest value on the amassing of factual data of all sorts. It is at one and the same time ambivalent about history and, in its expectations for the future, an exemplar of "whiggish" or progressive history.

All these factors prompt the question of whether neorealism is a theory consistent with the facts most relevant to its purposes and whether as it departs from history it meets the empirical tests for such a theory. A further question is whether neorealism is logically consistent within the framework it seeks to establish. Curiously, Waltz never asks himself this question or other questions related to the issue of internal consistency. Having disposed of human nature and the state as *primary* causes of war and anarchy because no single factor can play this role, he assigns the selfsame role to structure and the state system. He derives causation from the system, often in mechanical and automatic terms, whereas he had insisted earlier that causation could not be derived from human nature or the state. The system becomes a deus ex machina that spins off the attributes of the international system, including alliances, balances of power, or the status quo. Does this form of theory overlook the self-conscious role of states and individuals, as with Britain as the balancer in the nineteenth century or Bismarck as the consummate executor of the balance?

In his final chapter, Waltz does look to the future. Having insisted on the separation of history and theory, he introduces contemporary history by the back door. It is history, however, to fit the structure he has earlier created—a system of states overseen by the bipolar managers. Waltz brings his theory into line with the more fashionable trends in the discipline when he introduces an idea congenial to rational choice theory, that of collective good. Whereas realism has used the concept of mutual interests as the driving force inspiring states to affect the common good, as in the Marshall Plan, Waltz sees the two superpowers in the 1970s, and in particular the United States, shouldering the burdens of the state system in the name of the common good. "The greater the relative size of a unit, the more it identifies its own interest with the interest of the system."[16] They want the system to be orderly and peaceful and ensure that common interests are provided for. This is especially true of the transformation or maintenance of the system, the preservation of peace, and the management of common economic and other problems.

The United States justified its actions in two ways. It exaggerated the danger of the Soviet or Communist threat and, as with the domino theory, acted militarily on the periphery of the system. Or the country acted for the good of others inspired by its own version of what was good for them. Waltz seems to assume that the Soviets would do the same, although with far fewer capabilities.

Power is a concept that troubles Waltz. Power, he suggests, is too often seen as control, yet the use of military power seldom brings control. As he concludes his discussion, however, he writes, "Control rather than precise regulation and prevention rather than coordination . . . are the operations of key importance. To interdict the use of force by the threat of force, to oppose force with force . . . continue to be the most important means of control in security matters."[17] Two contradictions may be noted: first, he apparently calls upon the state, long subordinated to the system, to save the system; second, what are we to make of the fact that the other superpower in conflicts such as the Korean War seemed determined, Waltz's thesis notwithstanding, to alter rather than preserve the system by driving the United States from South Korea? (Recent Soviet and Korean documents make clear that the Soviets played a far more active role than had been assumed in calling signals and triggering action in the North Korean invasion.) Although it is doubtless possible for neorealists to explain such contradictions to their satisfaction, questions surely can be raised about the logical consistency of the framework Waltz establishes.

16. *Ibid.*, 198.
17. *Ibid.*, 207.

This having been said, Waltz's *Theory of International Politics* is a major contribution to the literature of international relations with which tomorrow's theorists must come to terms. It builds on his earlier work but goes beyond it. It constitutes the most important work thus far of systemic theory. The question is whether the past efforts of writers such as Morgenthau and Niebuhr, which represent attempts to be more systematic, are superior because they recognize the limits of theory and are more comprehensible and relevant. The earlier writings of the two that we have studied suggest this may be the case. It is difficult to see how the elaborate conceptual structure Waltz constructs serves his ends better than historical and political analysis. The main virtue of neorealism is that it concentrates attention on science and theory building. Its limitations stem from the resistance of the substance of international relations to such theories. Thus we return to those writers whose work continues to illuminate the subject for generations to come.

I have written elsewhere about the realists and the consistency of realist thought. The core question is whether realist thought follows logically from its premises. As with the founders who forged a constitution based on the separation of powers and checks and balances, present-day realists believe that an imperfect world is the result of forces inherent in human nature and that these forces seek balance internationally. The task of the statesman is to work with such forces, not against them. Because rivalry and conflict are a permanent part of the political landscape, the quest for goals and moral principles goes on in a political context in which imperfect individuals and states pursue their most vital interests. Moral principles can be approximated in the political arena but never fully realized. The concept of balancing interests and power is universal in all pluralist societies. Realism goes back to historical precedent rather than abstract reasoning and to human nature seeking its ends in the political process.

By the 1980s and 1990s, it was clear that realism had met the empirical test. The facts quite plainly lent themselves to the interpretation that realism put upon them. As the struggle for power continued in the Cold War era and with different characteristics in the post–Cold War era, few would question that the precepts of realism corresponded with the facts of international relationships. Nor was it to be doubted that the theory was consistent within itself. At the same time, realists recognized the limitations of any theory given the accidents and contingencies of history. Thus the theory endures which is consistent with the facts and with forces that are present in human nature reflected in competing goals and interests on the political scene. Because realism does not exclude history or shun the connection between theory and practice, it deals in a more fundamental way with human nature and politics, aspirations and the political process, and the relevance of its underlying premises about man, politics, and international politics—the subject of this book.

REALISM, IDEALISM, AND CYNICISM

We conclude our discussion with a reexamination of realism and idealism. Reinhold Niebuhr warned realists of the perils of cynicism and idealists of the dangers of innocence and illusions, the collapse of which led to cynicism. Future historians will almost certainly be perplexed by the unsettled mood of Americans in the 1990s following on the collapse of the Berlin Wall and the apparent demise of international communism. We tell ourselves that the victory of democracy over communism should have prompted a different response. Our perplexity over the loss of self-confidence is greater because the mood of Americans today follows a cyclical pattern. Over time, the focus of our discontent has been directed alternately to liberals and conservatives, presidents and the Congress, the nation and the states, Wall Street and bureaucracy, the media and lobbyists, churches and schools, legislators and judges, lawyers and elected officials, pollsters and pundits, owners and baseball players, government officials and businessmen. Cynicism feeds on itself. It spreads like a blanket covering a host of legitimate interests and relationships. It includes individuals and institutions across a broad spectrum. No one is immune. The public's doubts cast a threatening shadow over the nation's ability to confront new challenges.

Watergate and Vietnam

Some observers go back to Watergate and Vietnam to discover the origins of our discomfort. We ask how trust in a president is possible after President Nixon's deception. If a leader with experience in both branches of Congress and the presidency and vice-presidency betrays his oath to defend the Constitution, what can be expected of less-gifted successors? To forgive a president who misleads the people in the name of national security is one thing. To excuse lying and a persistent cover-up of a third-rate break-in is something else. The gulf between a president who waged two successful campaigns for "forgotten Americans" and one who not only forgot a crime but obstructed justice proved in the end impassable, even for Nixon's most loyal friends and supporters. What are we to think of a political system that elevates public figures so lacking in integrity and judgment? Or of young people who in opposing Nixon went further and proclaimed that they were giving the system only one more chance? New and more extreme forms of questioning continue in the present, even as silence has fallen over those who voiced doubts about American society following Watergate and Vietnam.

If Watergate illustrates the risks of cynicism, Vietnam is an example of the perils of utopianism or idealism. In the wake of the carnage and devastation of World War II, leaders renewed the call for an end to war. Some found the answer in collective security or in the international community stamping out the fires of aggression at its source. The defenders of collective security argued that the lesson of World War II was that appeasing an aggressor only led to the spreading of conflict and to an eventual worldwide conflagration. The United Nations invoked the Uniting for Peace procedures in the Korean War, but while more than fifty member nations approved the action, only a handful carried out its military requirements. Later, the United Nations chose not to act in Vietnam. The American decision to intervene was based on the SEATO treaty and a protocol interpreted as covering cases such as Vietnam. Although the spokesmen for collective security distinguished between universal and regional collective security, they included both as examples of the concept of "all for one and one for all." In retrospect, the failure of the idea of collective security or collective response to aggression in Vietnam resulted from an excessive idealism and the belief that nations were prepared to set aside their own strategic interests in meeting aggression wherever and whenever it occurred. In the end, the United States overreached the resolve of the American people to support a military action far from its shores and with the extent of its interests in dispute. Vietnam demonstrated the limits of the collective ideal.

Looking back, collective security had been heralded as the surest route to world peace and a detour around the troublesome constraints of national security. Solidarists assured the people that nations would commit a fraction of their military power to collective enforcement measures, at least on some limited basis. So convinced were its champions and defenders that they seldom used the term *national interest*. The reader will perhaps forgive a personal reference that may illustrate the divergence of thinking. On hearing of a dinner to which Reinhold Niebuhr and then-Rockefeller Foundation president Dean Rusk had both been invited, I conspired with the hosts to seat the two together at the head table. After the dinner, I had occasion to ask about their meeting, and they offered the same response: "I couldn't understand what he was driving at." In post–World War II years, there were few instances of a meeting of the minds of realists like Niebuhr and collective-security enthusiasts such as Rusk. Had there been more mutual understanding, the tragedy of Vietnam might have been averted.

The aftereffects of Watergate in particular continued far longer and with greater intensity because of American exceptionalism. From the beginning, European friends saw Watergate as one more political scandal to be taken in stride. They failed to understand the longlived character of the American dream and the vision of "a people on a hill." The United States saw itself as a beacon light of freedom and justice in the world. Crèvecoeur had compared the makers of American history with the artist who traces patterns on a landscape covered with new frost. We sketched in the design of a new world order. We were not as other people. An island nation surrounded by two great oceans with weaker neighbors to the north and south, we were safeguarded from the temptations of centuries of European powers. Watergate and Vietnam left a deep gash on the credibility of American exceptionalism. Because we took pride in our virtue, we suffered a deep loss with its passing.

Presidents and the Persistence of Cynicism

In the presidencies that followed Nixon, the nation struggled to regain its self-esteem, only to fall back from its advance. The task of

Nixon's successor, Gerald Ford, was to heal the nation, and he moved along that path. His appointments were men and women of quality. No president displayed greater mastery of the federal budget. In the Congress he had gained the trust and respect of colleagues on both sides of the aisle. As a midwesterner and former University of Michigan football player, he conveyed a sense of elemental strength and character. Yet for many, the confidence and goodwill he had gained in the relatively brief time span of his presidency was shattered by his pardon of Nixon.

Jimmy Carter followed Ford as president, and few questioned his convictions or his religious faith. He became a champion of human rights, and he brought the leaders of Israel and Egypt together at Camp David, where they achieved a limited Middle East peace settlement. He completed the negotiations that others had begun on the Panama Canal Treaty and made provisions for the transfer of power to the government of Panama. Carter undertook to help Americans stand for something in the world after what he considered had been the cynical realpolitik of Nixon and Kissinger. He quoted Reinhold Niebuhr on love and justice in his acceptance speech at the Democratic National Convention, but Niebuhrians questioned whether he understood the full import of Niebuhr's thought. In his words, if not in his actions, Carter was too moralistic in the first half of his administration to be a full-fledged Niebuhrian. Then he made a turn and a note of cynicism crept into his discourse when he praised the Shah of Iran and overlooked his human-rights record. Having proclaimed at the beginning of his administration that the threat of communism was exaggerated, he reversed himself after Afghanistan, rejecting American participation in the Olympics and sharply cutting back on Soviet agricultural assistance. The focus of much of the criticism of Carter was not on his goals—which many shared—but on his ineptitude in pursuing them.

All this reached its climax with Carter's handling of the Iranian hostage crisis, especially in public reaction to his controversial strategies, such as his promise not to use force against Iran. That promise removed Iran's incentive to release the hostages. The irony of Carter's decline is twofold: first, skilled negotiators such as Warren Christopher and Lloyd Cutler in Washington worked tirelessly to negotiate release of the hostages. The announcement of the agreement by the

Iranians was, however, held up until the day of President Reagan's inauguration. Second, the Carter human-rights program, much like Carter's image as an ex-president, has grown in acceptance, garnering the respect of conservatives and liberals alike in successive administrations. It can be argued that Carter has had an impact in reducing some of the cynicism in American society more through his legacy than by his words and actions in office.

Ronald Reagan's legacy is associated with the optimism he restored to American society. "Morning in America" became a reality for Republicans and Reagan Democrats who were inspired by "the Great Communicator." He helped rekindle the flames of patriotism through firmness with the Soviets and the greatest military buildup in history. His tax cuts pleased those in society who benefited most, and in the spirit of the times, Reagan did not call for sacrifice but accepted immediate gratification. The early successes of supply-side economics obscured its weaknesses as a viable economic theory. As has been true of leaders throughout history who have escaped death, Reagan's stature was enhanced by his courage and good humor during what his medical history reveals was a close brush with death. But the national debt grew to a record four trillion dollars during his administration, and his handling of the Iran-Contra scandal brought back memories of the Watergate cover-up. The optimism he engendered gave way to mixed feelings as Americans measured the consequences of his policies and his actions.

George Bush was the quintessential foreign-policy president, and his success in forming a coalition of nations to fight and finance the Gulf War was a landmark achievement. Because he was a pragmatist who proceeded step by step, he de-emphasized what he called "the vision thing." After agreeing to a tax increase despite his promise at the Republican convention sealed with the words "Read my lips, no new taxes," he gradually lost favor. His preference for foreign over domestic policy became a liability when the economy fell into recession. His failure to campaign for the presidency until after Labor Day, whatever the reasons, left the impression of a passive leader who stood for American leadership in the world but little else.

For Bill Clinton the character issue has restricted his ability to reduce cynicism about politics. Although his successful presidential campaign led many to assume he would bring new vision to the presidency, he soon came under fire for choosing as a first legislative priority the issue of gays in the military. That choice merely highlighted his lack of military service and was followed by a variety of scandals involving Cabinet and White House officials and events that took place when he was governor of Arkansas. Faced with a series of extraordinarily difficult problems, including the deficit and national debt, coupled with seemingly insoluble foreign-policy situations such as Bosnia, he searched for new strategies and answers. Even when he succeeded in bringing down the deficit and formulated successful American policies for Russia and international trade, he was criticized for "flip-flopping" in decision making and for lacking convictions.

Thus, none of the presidents after Nixon have succeeded in removing the cloud of cynicism about politics that now hangs over the country. This cynicism was accentuated by episodes such as the Post Office scandal, which involved congressional leaders. Yet reported misdeeds and problems of character and consistency, coupled with leaders' personal problems with alcohol and infidelity, have a long history. In looking for the cause of the public's loss of trust in its leaders, one must go back at least to Watergate and Vietnam. It would be false to see those debacles as a single cause of the problem, but where politics is concerned, they clearly served to trigger public reactions affecting the credibility of leaders.

Television and Cynicism

If political events such as Watergate and Vietnam have bred cynicism in American politics, novel institutions that have appeared on the national and international horizons and been advertised as the route to a brave new world have also played a part. Nationally, the powerful institution of television has profoundly influenced American politics, but not in ways that its defenders forecast. Internationally, the League of Nations and the United Nations were heralded as harbingers of perpetual peace. Instead, they became the focal point of political controversy. Claims concerning their role vastly exceeded reality.

The subject of television and politics has become an issue, on the national level, generating mounting concern. The gulf between the promise of television and its performance well illustrates the hazards of political prediction. In the post–World War II era, the communication revolution was widely touted as an instrument for bringing people and nations together. Once we were able to transport ourselves through the medium of television into the sanctum sanctorum of the political process, respect and support for government would spread across the land. Citizens had a right to know, and an explosion in information promised a new world of understanding. Precisely the opposite has happened, however, and we ask ourselves where this highly optimistic prediction went wrong. What is it about communication between people that produces not understanding but hostility and tension?

The late Karl Deutsch, a leading authority on communication studies, found that too much familiarity with another people's culture and politics may breed contempt and misunderstanding. For example, the more contacts multiplied, the more the French saw the English as lacking in culture. In turn, the English came to view the French as immoral. We suffer today from a surfeit of data and statistics pulled together seemingly at random and producing confusion as often as understanding. More is involved, however, than overkill in providing information. Television has purposes that surpass the supplying of information. One such purpose is entertainment, and another is the sale of advertising. In particular, success in advertising depends more on attracting attention and generating action than on the pursuit of truth. Attention is focused on the sensational: exaggerated claims for products, scandals, crime, the rise and fall of high-profile Americans. Mistrust and cynicism—not mutual understanding—are the result.

Thus a medium that was counted on to elevate political discourse has brought it down to the lowest common denominator. It has thrown the spotlight on the least ennobling aspects of human life and left an impression that all our leaders possess feet of clay, not occasionally but always. Too often, television at best tells half the story. If someone has fallen from grace, the fall eclipses everything that has gone before and comes after. We are given a narrow snapshot constricting the fullness of the human drama, with all its intermingling of good and evil, success and failure, triumph and tragedy. It has lowered the human drama to a Hobbesian state of nature wherein life is indeed "poor, nasty, brutish, and short."

With politics, television has been especially destructive. For the citizen, it has substituted passivity for participation and scandal for substance. The bottom line in political campaigns has become affordable television time accompanied by skyrocketing costs and simplified verbal messages. Door-to-door canvassing of voters has virtually disappeared. A hard-pressed electorate, finding themselves more and more remote from the political process, are reduced to judging their leaders on the basis of a steady stream of sound bites. They feed on a diet that producers sift out from a far more bounteous table of ideas. In one respect, the experience is nothing new. Who among us, beholden to trusted columnists who interpret in our behalf, can pretend to have ourselves truly known political leaders? Yet the knowledge to be gleaned from a fifteen-second quote predigested by a television technician pales into insignificance alongside a full-page column by a lifelong student of politics whose views compete on the same page with those of another lifetime student. Is it any wonder that once present-day leaders come to power, their conduct in office resembles scarcely at all the picture in the minds of voters, whose image of them is fashioned out of fragments preselected for their appropriateness for television? Not only has television failed to bring us closer to one another and to our leaders, it has also often distorted the picture in our minds of those leaders and realities. Discovering they have been misled on the ideas and character of their leaders, voters grow ever more cynical, and the cynicism expands to politics in general.

Of course, television is not alone in promoting cynicism. Ambition and greed surround and shape the approach to politics. The axiom that all is fair in love and politics is alive and well. It would be difficult, if not impossible, to claim that all the exigencies of seeking political office today have given us leaders who are the equal of the Founding Fathers. Even the number of candidates seeking federal judgeships has been reduced because of delays in the selection process, a pressing problem that a Miller Center commission has addressed. Long-accepted questionable practices, such as exploiting the resources of the congressional post office, only recently have come to light. Television, to its credit, has helped bring certain abuses to light. Yet these accomplishments are a far cry from the transforming power claimed for the power of television at its birth.

The United Nations: From Idealism to Cynicism

Institutions in the international arena have suffered a similar fate. The League of Nations was part of a combination of reforms promoted as the means of eliminating war among nations. The Kellogg-Briand Pact of 1928 pledged the nations of the world to outlaw war on the assumption that modern war had become unacceptable. With Hitler moving across Europe, however, it soon became evident that not the new institutions but the resolve of the major powers—France and England—was necessary to forestall a general war. The essential irrelevance of the League became increasingly self-evident when Emperor Haile Selassie called unsuccessfully on the organization to defend Ethiopia against invasion by Mussolini and Italy's Fascist troops. Europeans, especially, whose hopes for the League had been betrayed, lost faith and returned to alliances and regional approaches to international problems.

At the close of World War II, the United States led a crusade to establish a more powerful international organization whose major task was to guarantee international peace and security. Its architects crafted a U.N. charter that was stronger than that of the League. Chapter VI of the charter provided means for the peaceful settlement of disputes and Chapter VII for collective-security measures to enforce the peace. The latter's effectiveness in resolving great-power disputes was limited from the start by the veto. Collective actions against any of the five permanent members of the Security Council were subject to their negation.

From the outset it was clear that neither the Soviet Union nor the United States was prepared to undertake enforcement actions with others that affected their vital interests. Some secretaries-general were prepared to work within the limits of the charter, making use of the powers available to them for the peaceful resolution of disputes. They essentially abandoned the concept of collective security and adopted peacekeeping and mediation. Secretary-General Bhoutros Bhoutros-Ghali went further and proposed strategies for peacekeeping and for dozens of peacekeeping and even peacemaking missions around the world. At first, American support was forthcoming, but then a negative reaction set in. American taxpayers discovered that they were responsible for one-third of the U.N. budget. When

America sustained casualties during the United Nations' humanitarian intervention in Somalia, a cry went up against having U.S. troops serve under foreign commanders. Cynicism set in because the promise of an international organization that would take the place of national initiatives was being refuted. Americans discovered that the new international organization predicated on the idea of international cooperation was no substitute for sacrifice by sovereign states. Such sacrifices had to continue, but now were to be made within multinational institutions in which no individual nation's voice was controlling.

Having been led to believe that international institutions and what certain scholars called complex interdependence were taking the place of national policies and programs, Americans' discovery that national sacrifices were required to accomplish U.N. policies led to strong political reactions by a Republican congress. Legislation was proposed that not only sought to cut the percentage of U.S. support for the U.N. budget but also called for further reductions in proportion to the expenditures for U.S. troops serving under U.N. commanders. An optimistic view of the United Nations deteriorated into a cynical perspective regarding all actions, including those that fell far short of the collective-enforcement measures that were cause for the American and Soviet veto. The decline in American support is an example of idealism leading to disillusionment that is the final theme in our discussion of realism, idealism, and cynicism.

From Illusions to Disillusionment

Niebuhr's warning that realism runs the risk of spilling over into cynicism is well taken. At the same time, a realism that excludes the possibility of moral constraints on political action is actually cynicism or nihilism. Bismarck was a tough-minded realist, whereas the German Romanticists (such as Heinrich von Treischke, who glorified war as the highest end for men and nations) were cynics, even as the followers of Camus in a later period were nihilists. Unthinking idealism is a more common source of cynicism. In fact, true believers who embrace unrealistic goals experience frustration and disillusionment, the end product of which is cynicism. History makes clear that cynics more often than not are disappointed idealists who, having begun at one extreme on a spectrum extending from utopianism to cynicism, simply move to the other in reaction against the failure of their original extreme vision. Having embraced a political illusion and been disillusioned, they abandon all ideals that may prove illusory and embrace a philosophy that seeks to negate all values and ideals across the board.

As we have seen, the movement from one set of ideals to its opposite takes many forms. According to the dialectic, history moves from thesis to antithesis to synthesis, or from affirmation to negation to some kind of resolution. One extreme is challenged by another, and hope lies in a new configuration that reconciles the two. The resolution is only gradually realized, however, and the process may take decades or centuries to reach its final stage. In the instance of the dialectic at work in presidential succession, the movement from liberalism to conservatism was seen as requiring up to thirty years, even though a liberal—John F. Kennedy—became president after only eight years of conservatism under Dwight D. Eisenhower, and Ronald Reagan followed a liberal president—Jimmy Carter—who served only four years. The core idea of the cyclical view of politics is that the American voters grow weary or become disillusioned with representatives of one political philosophy and turn to its opposite in a more or less predictable period of time. They espouse one political ideology only to abandon it for a rival political creed that in turn invites disillusionment when it falls short of their expectations.

In the period between the two world wars, observers noted a somewhat similar process involving communism and fascism. Communism sought to take the place of liberalism. It constituted a reaction against the ideals of liberalism. As we have seen, liberalism stresses the sovereignty of the individual human being, whereas communism accents collectivities and social classes. It proposes a type of society and a type of man unlike any the world had seen in liberalism or in the political philosophies that preceded it. In the words of Michael Oakeshott, "It contained the most radical criticism that the Liberal Democratic doctrine has yet had to face." Communism appropriated some of the ideas of liberal democracy. "It preserved largely unchanged the most questionable element of Liberal Democracy, what may be called its moral ideal: 'the plausible ethics of productivity.'" Even as communism challenged liberalism, it embraced the primacy of economics as a determinant of politics. Oakeshott concluded, "It is the most complicated of all the doctrines . . . but it is never tired of proclaiming its simplicity; it makes a vast display of philosophical ideas, but it is full of self-contradictions; it is encumbered with a quaint medieval jargon but it . . . [became] the creed of millions."[18]

The other challenges to the ideals of Western civilization were fascism and German National Socialism. Once again, the economic and political crises in the United States and in European countries led to disillusionment with liberal democracy. Liberalism had served as the ideology that obscured the strivings for political dominance of the middle class. In its opposition to war, it removed some of the inspiring notions of glory and patriotism. It offered planning and order as substitutes for extreme individualism, which no one had practiced and believed in for more than fifty years, since the end of the nineteenth century. Yet "when Fascism comes to put something in its place we are given nothing better than what was rejected. . . . There may be something more inspiring in the materialism of Fascism, the materialism of an army and conquest, the materialism of a preference for methods of violence, than in the duller materialism of Liberal Democracy, but it is certainly not less materialistic." For those who were disillusioned by the dead weight of inflation, inefficiency, and unemployment, however, fascism for a brief moment in the stream of history was seen as offering an alternative. Nevertheless, it remained at best a doctrine of "cryptic statements and wide assertions."[19]

National socialism appeared to many, especially in Germany, to offer what fascism lacked. Despite the fierce nationalism it represented, it claimed a universal character not rooted in Hegel's world spirit but curiously reminiscent of it. It had the advantage of what seemed to the fearful a more coherent doctrine. Yet in the end, it was "merely a programme of power masquerading as a social ideal." Most of its tenets were not new. They belonged to a harsh tradition in German social and political thought. They were, however, held "with an unrivalled self-consciousness and an unmatched solem-

18. Michael Oakeshott, *The Social and Political Doctrines of Contemporary Europe* (New York, 1947), xx.

19. Nitze, *Tension Between Opposites,* xxi.

nity."[20] Its distinguishing doctrines were race and blood and *der Fuehrer*. The profound disillusionment of Germans with the Weimar Republic and liberal democracy and their inability to respond to economic and social crises made Nazism seem credible for its brief "Moment" in history.

Thus, belief in false ideals has led to disillusionment and the overthrowing of concepts grasped in a time of innocence. Cynicism about one set of ideals leads eventually to cynicism about another. Those who suffer disillusionment most consistently are the true believers. Putting their faith wholly and unqualifiedly in false gods, they lose all trust in gods who come in their wake. Prudence requires both greater awareness of the limits of idealism and its problematical fulfillment if cynicism is to be averted. In politics, the first law is that the morally desirable must be reconciled with the politically possible. It is never enough to affirm a faith. Someone must find a way to give it content in ever-changing circumstances. If illusions are not to lead inescapably to disillusionment, statesmen must formulate realizable aims and goals measured by real interests and proven capabilities. Realism is not the only path to formulate realizable aims and goals measured by interests and capabilities. Realism is not the only path to a viable politics. It is, however, generally the most attainable and best attuned to the world of practice. It can keep faith alive despite human frailties. It is able to reconcile interests and ethics.

20. Oakeshott, *The Social and Political Doctrines*, xxii.

EPILOGUE

No one can speak for all approaches and theorists of international relations. Each interpreter inescapably offers a view of the writings of others that is colored by deeply held beliefs and presuppositions. This book is no exception, even though I have tried to maintain balance. My defense is that subjectivity is no vice if readers recognize it for what it is.

Political realism provides a definable ground of analysis. Its principles are not obscure. It puts national interest first and assumes rivalries among nations. Against the background of realism we have tried to trace the origins and unfolding of international studies, including an array of differing schools of thought.

I have lived through most of the debate about schools of thought and hold views about the emerging theoretical perspectives and those who developed them. Therefore, readers have found criticism in the preceding pages. In my view, criticism invites counter-criticism and response. Unless I am mistaken, a book of this kind will be answered, and this can be an important outcome of my inquiry. Put simply, others will answer my assertions, and this is as it should be.

Having said that, let me also say that I am concerned with the random choices being made in some discussions of international relations. Some of those approaches are not, shall we say, "dry behind the ears." Novelty ought not be assumed to qualify short-lived inquiries as equal in merit with lifelong studies. The treatise I read over and over again was first published in 1948; much of today's discussion centers on works that live on to provoke debate. There must be a reason why some studies endure and others pass from view almost before they are formally recognized.

If I have stirred readers to think and challenge others, one of my purposes will have been served. I hope we can continue to pursue new and old ideas. If some also find in my words an invitation to seek understanding at a deeper level, another goal will have been realized. This book is a plea that students search for interrelatedness among concepts, attitudes, orientations, and philosophies. Finally, it appeals to readers not to abandon approaches that have survived strenuous criticism and debate. To abandon a good school of thought would be far worse than never to have undertaken to establish structures and principles of thought.

I feel confident that over time we can look forward to new and innovative approaches. Even then, however, I believe that some of the traditional schools of thought will continue to illuminate thinking in international relations.

INDEX

Acheson, Dean: 106; and Holmes, 54; and Nitze, 58; on the role of theory, 42, 69

American exceptionalism: 147; and realism, 111, 113; and Woodrow Wilson, 114–15

Aquinas, Thomas, 20

Aristotle, 20, 61, 64

Aron, Raymond, 77

Atlantic Charter, 81

Augustine, St., 20, 61, 131, 137

Austrian school of thought, 3

Balance of power theory: 142; and Hume, 137; and Vagts, 129, 137

Bargaining theory, 129

Berdahl, Clarence, 26

Berlin, Isaiah, 65

Bhoutros-Ghali, Bhoutros, 153

Bismarck, Otto von, 131, 136, 142, 154

Bohlen, Charles: 65; and NSC-68, p. 57; and theory versus practice, 77

British Committee on the Theory of International Relations, 107, 140

Brodie, Bernard, 32

Brownlow, Louis, 11, 25

Bull, Hedley, 109

Bunche, Ralph, 27

Bundy, McGeorge, 28

Burckhardt, Jakob, 50

Bush, George: 149; and new world order, 6, 7, 81–82; and United Nations, 82

Butterfield, Sir Herbert: 7; and British Committee on the Theory of International Relations, 107, 140; *Diplomatic Investigations,* 108; and Gifford Lectures, 107; influenced by Niebuhr, 106–107; and optimism, 73; *Origins of Science,* 108; and realism, 140–41; on role of theory, 41; protégé of Temperley, 107

Carr, E. H.: on force, 78; and Marxism, 93; and realism, 94; *The Twenty Years' Crisis,* 7

Carter, Jimmy, 7, 80, 148–49

Christian realism: and Niebuhr, 105; and realism, 9, 53. *See also* Realism

Churchill, Winston, 69, 78

City University of New York, 3, 90

Claude, Inis, 27

Clausewitz, Karl von, 138

Clayton, Will, 56–57, 60

Clinton, William: 150; and cynicism, 149; and new world order, 82–83

Cold War: 138, 143, 144; and deterrence, 6; end of, 74, 80, 145

Collective security, 81, 146–47

Cologne School, 9

Columbia University: and Fox, 129; and Tannenbaum, 8, 111; War and Peace Institute at, 129

Communism: and Leites, 14; versus liberalism, 155; and Niebuhr, 97–99. *See also* Marxism; Socialism

INDEX

84–85; at Harvard, 26; and Wright, 14. *See also* Legalism
International Court of Justice, 120
International Organization, 29
International relations: and collective security, 146–47; and hierarchy, 127; and idealism, 125–26, 154–55; and international regimes, 122; normative, 3, 4; and power, 122; and vulnerability, 122; and war, 135

Jackson, Robert, 17
Jay, John, 136
Johnson, Lyndon B., 81
Johnson, Walter, 14
Judgment, 115–16
Just-war theory, 93, 108

Kant, Immanuel, 130, 133, 134, 135
Kaplan, Morton, 139, 140
Kellogg-Briand Act, 153
Kelsen, Hans, 27, 136
Kennan, George F.: 44, 46, 106; *American Diplomacy,* 45, 60, 62; and Aristotle, 61; *Around the Cragged Hill,* 4, 47, 48; *At a Century's Ending,* 4; and Augustine, 61; and containment, 47; and human nature, 49–53; and "Long Telegram," 57; and Machiavelli, 61; *Memoirs,* 4; and morality, 62; and Niebuhr, 141; and Nitze, 57, 60; and NSC-68, p. 57; and optimism, 74; and Policy Planning Staff, 5; and scientific approach, 48–49; and self-evaluation, 52; and role of theory, 69; and theory versus practice, 77; and World War I, 61
Kennedy, John F., 101
Keohane, Robert: 138; on interdependence, 120–24; *Power and Interdependence,* 120
Keynes, John Maynard, 6, 117–18
King, Martin Luther, 78
Kissinger, Henry, 108, 148
Knorr, Klaus, 32
Korean War, 80, 143, 146–47
Kuhn, Thomas, 141

Lasswell, Harold: 14; at Chicago, 13, 23; and Merriam, 11; and psychopathology, 12; and scientific approach, 22; at Yale Law School, 33
League of Nations, 4, 43, 88, 125, 126, 150, 153
Legalism, 45, 46. *See also* International law
Leiserson, Avery, 23
Leites, Nathan, 11, 14
Liberalism, 95–96, 155–56
Lincoln, Abraham, 69
Lippmann, Walter: 4, 106; *American Foreign Policy,* 44; on leadership, 44; and *New Republic,* 43, 96; and optimism, 74; and socialism, 96
Locke, John, 20
Logical positivism, 64
Luther, Martin, 131

Machiavelli, Niccolò, 61, 75, 138
Macrides, Roy, 134
Maistre, Joseph de, 65–66
Malthus, Thomas R., 92, 131
Marshall, C. B., 47, 77
Marshall, George C., 58–59
Marshall Plan, 57, 143
Marx, Karl, 133
Marxism, 93, 125–26. *See also* Communism; Marx, Karl; Socialism
Mason, Edward, 27
Mearsheimer, John, 35
Merriam, Charles: and Brownlow, 11; at Chicago, 10, 11, 12, 14; and Easton, 23; and Gosnell, 11, 21; and Lasswell, 11; and Leiserson, 23; and Leites, 11; and Morgenthau, 23; *New Aspects of Politics,* 11; and politics, 25; and Pritchett, 23; and Schuman, 11; and scientific approach, 21–22; and White, 11; and Wright, 11, 23
Metternich, Klemens von, 136
Metzler, Lloyd, 15
Millikan, Max, 27
Mitrany, David, 83–84, 120